THE HOUSE SERVANT'S DIRECTORY

THE HOUSE SERVANT'S DIRECTORY

An African American Butler's
1827 Guide

ROBERT ROBERTS

DOVER PUBLICATIONS, INC.
Mineola, New York

Bibliographical Note

This Dover edition, first published in 2006, is an unabridged republication of the work originally published in 1827 by Munroe and Francis,
Boston and Charles S. Francis, New York, under the title *The House
Servant's Directory, or a Monitor for Private Families: Comprising Hints on
the Arrangement and Performance of Servants' Work*. The Publisher's Note
has been specially prepared for this reprint.

The minor errors and inconsistencies found in the text are from the original edition, and remain unchanged here for the sake of authenticity.

International Standard Book Number: 0-486-44905-X

Manufactured in the United States of America
Dover Publications, Inc., 31 East 2nd Street, Mineola, N.Y. 11501

Publisher's Note

ROBERT Roberts, author of *The House Servant's Directory*, was one of the most prominent African-Americans of his time. Although much of his early life remains a mystery, including whether he was born free or a slave, it is known that he was born in Charleston, South Carolina between 1777 and 1780. When he arrived in Boston in 1805, he was able to read and write proficiently and had excellent skills as a domestic servant—skills that were in high demand in the North at this time, especially with the rise of wealthy, conservative Federalists and their country estates. It was thus easy for a man like Roberts to find gainful employment, and he did—working for a variety of aristocratic New Englanders for nearly a quarter century. His life changed dramatically in 1825, however, when he entered the service of his final and most illustrious employer, Christopher Gore (1758–1827). Gore, a former United States senator and governor of Massachusetts, was a leading Federalist who had built his country home, Gore Place, in Waltham in 1805–06. Gore Place was a sprawling estate; and by 1825, with Gore in declining health, a capable and experienced butler was desperately needed. Robert Roberts filled that need admirably, becoming Gore's right-hand man for almost two years and overseeing all aspects of the household's requirements.

After Christopher Gore's death on March 1, 1827, Robert Roberts never again worked as a domestic servant. While the reasons behind this are unclear, it was the profits from this book, *The House Servant's Directory*, that helped him support himself and his large family. Published less than two weeks after Gore's death, the work was, most likely, written with his knowledge and consent; and, likely too, that Gore contributed financially to its creation. In any event, *The House Servant's Directory* was among the first books written by an African-American author and printed by a commercial publishing house. It was also the product of many long years of experience as a servant, and the entire book reflects Roberts' abiding passion—to be the best employee that he could be, regardless of the task assigned. To him, no detail was too small to be ignored, no trifle too insignificant to be overlooked. The result was a book that would become the standard for household management for years to come.

As for Roberts, his remarkable career did not end here and he did not simply fade into obscurity. He devoted the remaining thirty-three years of his life to his family, his church, and the abolitionist cause, ceaselessly fighting to expand the rights of African-Americans in both the North and the South, and leading his Boston community against the then-popular Back-to-Africa Movement. When Robert Roberts died in 1860 (somewhere in his early eighties), he was among the wealthiest African-Americans in Boston and an early black landowner. He was mourned in the city not only as the author of a remarkable book, but also as a pioneer in race relations who helped breach the divide through dignity, intelligence, and an almost puritanical belief in the nobility of service and hard work.

—JAMES D. MILLER

THE
HOUSE SERVANT'S DIRECTORY,
OR
A MONITOR FOR PRIVATE FAMILIES :
COMPRISING
HINTS ON THE ARRANGEMENT AND PERFORMANCE OF
SERVANTS' WORK,
WITH GENERAL RULES FOR
SETTING OUT TABLES AND SIDEBOARDS
IN FIRST ORDER ;
THE ART OF WAITING
IN ALL ITS BRANCHES ; AND LIKEWISE HOW TO CONDUCT
LARGE AND SMALL PARTIES
WITH ORDER ;
WITH GENERAL DIRECTIONS FOR PLACING ON TABLE
ALL KINDS OF JOINTS, FISH, FOWL, &c.
WITH
FULL INSTRUCTIONS FOR CLEANING
PLATE, BRASS, STEEL, GLASS, MAHOGANY ;
AND LIKEWISE
ALL KINDS OF PATENT AND COMMON LAMPS :
OBSERVATIONS
ON SERVANTS' BEHAVIOUR TO THEIR EMPLOYERS ;
AND UPWARDS OF
100 VARIOUS AND USEFUL RECEIPTS,
CHIEFLY COMPILED
FOR THE USE OF HOUSE SERVANTS ;
AND IDENTICALLY MADE
TO SUIT THE MANNERS AND CUSTOMS OF FAMILIES
IN THE UNITED STATES.

By ROBERT ROBERTS.

WITH
FRIENDLY ADVICE TO COOKS
AND HEADS OF FAMILIES,
AND COMPLETE DIRECTIONS HOW TO BURN
LEHIGH COAL.

BOSTON,
MUNROE AND FRANCIS, 128 WASHINGTON-STREET.
NEW YORK,
CHARLES S. FRANCIS, 189 BROADWAY.
1827.

THIS valuable Work was written by a servant in one of the most respectable families in this city, the demise of whose very honourable head, with deep regret we have to record while penning this advertisement; and we hope it will be some recommendation to this useful book, to give an extract of a letter which we received from the late Hon. CHRISTOPHER GORE, a few weeks before his decease.

"I have read the work attentively, and think it may be of much use. The directions are plain and perspicuous; and many of the recipes I have experienced to be valuable. Could servants be induced to conform to these directions, their own lives would be more useful, and the comfort and convenience of families much promoted. Consider me as a subscriber for such number of copies as six dollars will pay for, and I think that many more would be subscribed for in Boston."

Numerous other recommendations could have been procured, but this we deem sufficient.

If the public have applauded Dr. Kitchener for improving the minutiæ and economy of the larder, what praise is not due to an humble attempt to amend the morals and awkwardness of domestics? In school-learning generally our native servants surpass foreigners, but in manner, deportment, and a knowledge of the duties of their station, it must be admitted they are considerably inferior. To borrow a phrase from the kitchen, our aboriginal servants need *grilling*; they require much instruction, and an apprenticeship to the art and faculty of *unbending*. Like certain "woollens imported in a raw state," noticed in a late congressional debate, it is requisite in order to giving them a proper gloss and finish, to send them to a "brushing establishment."

It cannot be denied that many of our servants, whilst perfectly willing to receive their wages, are either unwilling to submit to the powers that be, by fulfilling the duties for which such wages were stipulated, or from gross ignorance of domestic concerns, are totally unfit for service. An attempt to amend these matters by one from among their own number deserves, and we hope will receive the approbation and patronage of all aggrieved, so far at least as presenting a copy of this work to every house servant.

As to the Receipts for expurgating lamps, forks, and boots, compounding liquids, powders, &c. &c. given in this book, although like the author of the Cook's Oracle we cannot say we have actually *eaten* each one, having neither the necessary dyspeptic qualifications of the ostrich, nor the gusto of the Esquimaux or Kamschadale, yet, being assured by the author that he has himself operated on all of them, and on hundreds of others not set down because not infallible, we believe they will be found of essential service, and accordingly recommend them, when needed, to notice and use.

The publishers have in some sort amended the orthography and punctuation; otherwise the book is printed from the author's notes, "verbatim et literatim." No apology is necessary for thus presenting it, as the perceptions of some of its intended readers are a little obtuse, and it is requisite to give them line upon line, in something of the Dogberry style. Different views of the same object are taken, to enforce the fact more strongly on the recollection, and our author, as a servant, speaks to the comprehension of his fellow servants, without more diffuseness than answers the intended purpose.

In fine, this book is just such an one as has been long wanted, emanating from just the right quarter, and written precisely as might be wished: and with these few words of prologue we permit the author to speak for himself.

Boston, March 1, 1827.

INDEX

INTRODUCTION

IN the first place, I shall address myself to my young friends
Joseph and David, as they are now about entering into
gentlemen's service, which they will find in course of time a very
critical station for them to fulfil in its proper order; therefore I
most sincerely intreat them to practice and study these few
directions and observations, which I have laid down in the
following pages, for their benefit and instruction, likewise for
the benefit of those families whom they may have the honour
to serve.

Besides, there are many young men who are in good situations at present, but who oftentimes are deficient of some of the
several branches that are requisite for a perfect servant to
understand; I therefore have a sincere wish to serve all those
who are in that capacity of earning an honest living, and perhaps
are not perfect in the several branches of their business, which
in this station they are expected to perform, without being
ordered by the lady of the family. There are many young men
who live out in families, who, I am sorry to say, do not know how
to begin their work in proper order unless being drove by the
lady of the family, from one thing to another, which keeps them
continually in a bustle and their work is never done.

There is no servant that can keep from being in a state of confusion, that has not a regular rule for his work, and, on the other
hand, how disagreeable it must be for the lady, who has to tell
them every thing that she wants to be done. It was merely for
this idea, that the author of this took in hand to lay before the
public those general rules and directions for servants to go by as
shall give satisfaction to their employers, and gain a good reputation for themselves. And it is my most earnest wish to give to
the utmost extent of my power, every instruction that is requisite for a house servant to understand.

11

Now, my young friends, you must consider that to live in a gentleman's family as a house servant is a station that will seem wholly different from any thing, I presume, that ever you have been acquainted with; this station of life comprises comforts, privileges, and pleasures, which are to be found in but few other stations in which you may enter; and on the other hand many difficulties, trials of temper, &c. more perhaps than in any other station in which you might enter, in a different state of life. Therefore, my young friends, when you hire yourself to a lady or gentleman, your time or your ability is no longer your own, but your employer's; therefore they have a claim on them whenever they choose to call for them: and my sincere advice to you is, always to study to give general satisfaction to your employers, and by so doing you are sure to gain credit for yourself.

Now, Joseph, I am going to make a few observations to you.— In the first place, my young friend, the various stations of life are appointed by that Supreme Being, who is the giver of all goodness; therefore every station that he allows us to fulfil, is useful and honorable in their different degrees: for instance we find from history and holy writ, that domestic servants have frequently been intrusted with matters of the greatest importance to their employers. Of this we have a memorable instance of your namesake Joseph, who was sold by his brethren to the Ishmaelites, and bought by Potiphar to be his domestic servant, and in this capacity Joseph acquitted himself with honesty and integrity, and his master saw that the Lord was with him, and that the Lord prospered all that was about him; and the Lord blessed the Egyptian's house for Joseph's sake. And he left all that he had in Joseph's care, and he knew not aught he had, save the bread that he did eat.—Genesis, chapter 39th. I might mention in another instance the fidelity of Mordecai, who, in his capacity as a porter to King Ahasuerus, saved that monarch from the violent hands of his two chamberlains.

Happy, my young friends, are those families that have servants who study the comfort and welfare of their employers, and who in return do the same by them! The kind admonitions of a good and affectionate mistress or master should always be listened to with respect and obedience, for the wise man saith, "As

an ear-ring of gold, so is a wise reproof upon an obedient ear."—
Proverbs xxiv, 12. In the next place, my young friends, you may
perhaps find a master or a mistress who may act unkindly and
unjustly towards you, as Laban did to Jacob his servant and son-
in-law; but if you do your duty honestly and faithfully, depend
on it that you will be more happy in your integrity than your
employers can be in their injustice; for it is much better to be
the oppressed than to stand in the place of the oppressor; for
patience is ever acceptable in the sight of God, and in due time
will be rewarded, because God hath promised that it shall be so;
and when have his promises failed? Jacob's master shifted and
shuffled him about for twenty years; and changed his wages ten
different times, yet the Lord blessed the honest and upright
servant, because he had done that which was just, between his
master and himself. Let those considerations, my young friends,
ever stimulate your minds to truth and faithfulness, in all your
situations through life, and God will guide and prosper you in all
your undertakings.

I know there are many temptations to lead young men to their
ruin; but you should be very cautious of what company you
keep. How many young men in our station of life have come to
their ruin by keeping bad company, and neglecting the business
of their employers; so, my young friends, I tell ye to beware of
all bad habits, such as drinking, gambling, swearing, telling
falsehoods, and wasting your time when sent out on the business
of your employers; for this is not your time you spend, but your
employer's, for all your time belongs to them.

Remember, my young friends, that your character is your
whole fortune through life; therefore you must watch over it
incessantly, to keep it from blemish or stain; for without character it is useless to seek after any respectable service whatever.
Nor can I wonder at ladies and gentlemen for the minute
inquiries that they make, in every point, of a stranger's character. How many instances have we all heard of masters being
robbed by dishonest servants, and their very existence exposed
to imminent danger through evil connections being formed,
unknown to them, by the inmates of their house. Remember
also, that if you keep company with those whose character is not

of the best, your character will be censured as much in a manner as though you were as bad as themselves; for our good Saint Paul says, that evil communications corrupt good manners;—for the wicked favour the wicked, and the good favour the good; neither flatter any body, nor suffer any one to flatter thee.

There are a few more things which I shall caution you against. Remember always to govern thy tongue and passions, when thou art angry with any person; for anger will hurt you more than injury; and my kind advice to you is, never to be a slave to passion. Besides, the law of nature forbids us to do injury to one another; God hath given nothing to man which can be compared to reason and wisdom. Always strive to relieve those who are in distress, if it is in your power, for the christian religion not only commands us to help our friends, but to relieve our greatest enemies; for so we shall make them our friends; and shall promote love, kindness, peace and good will among men. It concerns all men to help the miserable. It is the property of a little mind to flatter the rich; for flattery can hurt nobody but whom it pleases. The desire of riches, glory, and pleasure, are diseases of the mind; but the power of honesty is so great, that we should love it even in our greatest enemy. Virtue procures and preserves friendship, but vice produceth hatred and quarrels.

Now, my young friends, Joseph and David, I again for the last time most sincerely intreat you both to devote your attention to the following pages, in which I have laid down such rules and regulations for the convenience of your work, and the fulfilment of your several duties to your employers, as from my own long experience as a house servant in some of the first families in England, France, and America, will prove very beneficial to you and the public. Not that I mean to offer them as a fixed standard; because almost every family differs in the execution of their domestic affairs, and it is the duty of a good servant to do things in that way that his employers like best. But my idea of publishing this was for a general guide, and to afford an insight into matters connected with gentlemen's families; and I have always found those arrangements, which I have prescribed in the following pages, very satisfactory to those ladies and gentlemen whom I have had the honour to serve. But it is true, I have had many difficulties and trials of temper to encounter; but I have always viewed them as appointed by that Supreme Being whose goodness is ever bestowed upon those who bear every trial and difficulty with patience and obedience.

My young friends, I hope you will pardon me for dwelling so long on these subjects; but many, very many, have I known whose prospects in early life, and all their enjoyments, have been blasted by not attending to good advice. How many have we seen going about a city, like vagabonds, diseased in mind and body, and mere outcasts from all respectable society, and a burthen to themselves, therefore I sincerely wish that my young friends may fulfil their several duties with honesty, integrity, and due respect to their employers and fellow servants in general; and I shall now conclude my general exhortations for your welfare, and enter on the particular statements respecting your domestic duties, &c.

THE BENEFIT OF EARLY
RISING TO SERVANTS

IN order to get through your work in proper time, you should make it your chief study to rise early in the morning; for an hour before the family rises is worth more to you than two after they are up; for in this time you can get through the dirtiest part of the work, which you cannot well do after the family rises; for then you always are liable to interruption; therefore by having the dirtiest part of your work executed, it will prove a very great comfort to you. As there is nothing more disagreeable than to run about with dirty hands and dirty clothes; and this must inevitably be the case if you defer this part of your work until every body is stirring and bustling about.

In the next place, you must have a proper dress for doing your dirty work in; for you should never attempt to wait on the family in the clothes that you clean your boots, shoes, knives, and lamps in; for the dress that you wear to do this part of your work is not fit to wait in, on ladies and gentlemen.

There is no class of people to whom cleanliness of person and attire is of more importance than to servants in genteel families. There are many servants, whom I have been eye witness to, through negligence as I must call it, who are a disgrace to the family that they live with, as well as to themselves, by appearing in their dirty clothes at a time of day that they should have all the dirtiest part of their work done. Every man that lives in this capacity should have a sufficient quantity of clothes to appear always neat and respectable; both for his own credit, and for the credit of the family he serves; therefore I shall give you a few hints on what clothes are suitable for his different work. In the first place for doing your dirty work, you should have you a round-a-bout jacket of a dark colour, with overalls, or loose trowsers, of the same colour, with a vest, and a cap of some description to keep the dust from your hair, with a green baize

17

apron. This is a very suitable habiliment for your morning's work, that is, before your family come down to breakfast; at which time you should have on a clean shirt collar and cravat, with a clean round jacket, white linen apron and clean shoes, with your hair neatly combed out. This is a most neat and clean attire for serving breakfasts. You must always make your calculations what time it may take to get through your work, so as to clean yourself for breakfast.

In the next place, I shall give you some directions on your dress for dinner. You should make it a general rule always to have a good suit of clothes or two, for attending at dinner, as a servant should always at this time look neat and tidy, but not foppish; what I mean by being foppish is, to wear a great bunch of seals to your watch, and a great pin sticking out of your bosom. There is nothing looks more ridiculous than to see a servant puff out above his ability; it really puts me in mind of the fable of the frog and the ox; there are many, I know, who never think of laying by a little sum of money against the time of need, but spend it all, as fast as they earn it, on fine dress.

I never find fault with a man for dressing neat and plain; but to go beyond extremes is ridiculous; you should always have a good suit for dinner, and I shall here give you a few hints on a suit which is very genteel and becoming. For the winter season you should have comfortable clothing, such as a good superfine blue body coat, blue cassimere trowsers, and a yellow cassimere vest. This is a very neat and becoming dress to wait on dinner. You should have at least two or three suits of light clothes for the summer season; as they require to be changed once or twice per week, if they are light coloured; but black bombazine is preferable.

CLEANING BOOTS AND SHOES

As these things are often wanted in a hurry, therefore you should always have them in readiness, if possible. In this operation, you should always have good brushes and good blacking. These are implements that are indispensably necessary; without which, no credit will be given to the operator. In the first place you must remove all the dirt from your boots or shoes, with your hard brush. When perfectly clean you must stir up your blacking with a stick, then apply a little on your black brush, and apply it lightly and smoothly over your boots or shoes, then apply your polishing brush quick and lightly over them, and in a few minutes you will have a beautiful polish. Should any brown spots appear, which often do, by not putting on the blacking even, then apply your blacking brush lightly over it a second time, and by this process you will have a beautiful polish.

When you have ladies shoes to clean, be very clean and careful about them. As the linings are generally white, you must have clean hands, as the lining is apt to get soiled; some of these shoes are cleaned with milk, or the whites of eggs, such as Morocco, or any kind of glazed leather whatever. You must apply the mixture with a sponge, and lay them before the fire or in the sun to dry; then take a soft brush, or a silk handkerchief; this will give them a fine polish.

You will find it necessary, once in a while, to grease gentlemen's boots and shoes, especially in winter time, as the leather is apt to crack with the wet and cold. You will find, by referring to the Index, full directions for rendering boots and shoes perfectly water proof. I therefore proceed to the next branch of work that is requisite to get out of the way as early in the morning as possible.

CLEANING KNIVES

This is another branch of work that requires the greatest care and attention, as your best knives generally have to bear the inspection of a number of tasteful eyes during the course of dinner. Every servant should see that he has proper utensils to do his work with, as you cannot expect to do your work in proper order, if you have not the means to accomplish it with. How many good things are spoilt through bad management of the man, and the want of convenient tools to work with. Now, in order to clean knives and forks well, you must get you a soft pine plank or board; let it be free from knots, and about six feet long; have feet or standers under it, so as to raise it exactly to the height of your hips, as this is the proportion for you to bear a regular pressure on your knives; then have you a good soft Bristol brick, and rub it a few times up and down your board, then take a knife in each hand and stand opposite the centre of the board, with the backs of the knives towards the palms of your hands, then expand your arms, keeping the blades level on the board, with a quick motion draw your hands to and from you, frequently looking at the side you are scouring, to see when clean. Do not lean too heavy on the blades for fear of breaking them. In this mode you will soon grow tractable, and will shortly be able to clean two dozen where you would only clean one dozen by taking one knife at a time, and scouring it with your one hand. A good set of knives is a valuable thing, and soon spoiled if not properly taken care of by the man who has the charge of them. There is no branch of a servant's business that will gain more credit for him, from ladies of taste, than keeping his knives and forks in primo bono; as they have many spectators.

DIRECTIONS FOR CLEANING STEEL FORKS

The best method of cleaning steel forks, is to have a deep box or a small keg, the latter is preferable; fill it with fine sand and chopped hay or straw, either will answer the purpose. To do this perfectly, put some of your hay into the bottom of your keg, then put in some sand, and so on, until it is quite full, then press it close down, and wet it with water, to keep it damp, as it will have more effect in taking the black from off the prongs, as forks often are very black and hard to clean, after having been used in acids, &c.

When you clean them, take two in each hand, and stab them several times in the sand, and so on, until you have them all done; then have an old hard brush for the purpose of brushing the sand from between the prongs; likewise have a piece of buckskin, or an old glove, to polish them off with. This is the true and best method of cleaning steel forks.

Now I shall give you directions for cleaning the handles of your knives and forks, after the blades and prongs have all been cleaned. In the first place take a towel and immerse it in water, then wring it out all but dry; hold this towel in your right hand, with a dry knife towel in the left, to wipe the blade. When you have them all done, then give them a light rub over with a dry towel, including handles, &c. Should you have silver knives, you may clean them with a little gin and whiting mixed together, and rubbed over the handles when dry; if the handles be fluted, you must brush them with your plate brush, and polish with your shamois, or, as it is pronounced, shammy leather.

My young friend, I have always been thus particular about my knives and forks, because they are things that, from the appearance of which, not only the lady and gentleman of the family, but every one that sits down at table, forms an opinion of the cleanliness and good management of the servant to whose care they are intrusted; and I sincerely wish that you may gain the same approbation.

TRIMMING AND CLEANING LAMPS

Lamps are now so much in use for drawing-rooms, dining rooms, and entries, that it is a very important part of a servant's work to keep them in perfect order, so as to show good light. I have been in some houses where the rooms were almost filled with smoke and stench of the oil, and the glasses of the lamps clouded with dust and smoke, from the cottons being uneven, or left up too high; this is a very disagreeable thing indeed. But it is not always a servant's fault, for, unless there is good oil, and plenty of it allowed to the man, it is impossible for them to burn well. But it is a man's fault if they are dirty, or not in good order; and to remedy this disaster, when you first hire with a family, let it be your first object to examine all your lamps and see that they are all in order; and if not, let your employers know immediately, that is, if they are so bad that you cannot remedy them yourself, in which case they should be taken to some mechanist to be put in good order immediately.

When you have them in perfect order, by a little care and attention you can have very little trouble with them afterwards, in giving them a proper and thorough cleaning, which you should do at least once a fortnight. When you do this, take two or three quarts of soft boiling water, put into it two or three teaspoonsfull of pearl ashes, then empty your lamps, and take them all to pieces, observing where each particle belongs, that you may have no trouble in putting them together again. When you have them apart, first fill the cistern, that part which holds the oil, with this boiling water, and then shake it well; don't empty it into the rest of your water, for it will make it dirty. After this, if there should be any gum about them, scrape it off with an old knife, then put it into the tub which contains the rest of your water, and wash it well with a piece of old linen, which you must have for that purpose, with all the other parts likewise. When you have this all done, wipe them dry and put them before the fire or in the sun to dry; and when you have put them together, give them a good polish with a fine cloth or silk handkerchief.

You should wash your lamp glasses every morning, when you are washing your glasses or breakfast things, and put them by in their proper place until they are wanted.

You should always have a clean towel when you are lighting your lamps, in order to dust your lamp glasses before you put them on, as they will show much better light.

When you are cleaning or trimming your lamps in the morning, you should be very particular in emptying the dripper, or that part of the lamp that holds the droppings; for if this part is not kept clean to admit the air, the lamp will never burn well. You must likewise keep your lamp wicks in a dry place; this you may do by having a drawer, which you may keep for this purpose. When you put on fresh cottons, you must be very careful to put them on the thimble quite even. And likewise see that they fit exactly, or the cotton will slip from off the thimble when you go to raise it. You should never cut your cottons with scissors; it is much the best way to let down your oil, and light the cotton; when it burns a little so as to be even, blow it out, and rub off the snuff with a piece of paper even with the burner or socket, which contains the wick. You should always use wax tapers for lighting lamps, as paper generally flies about and makes dirt.

DIRECTIONS FOR CLEANING PLATE

This is another part of a house servant's work, which requires particular care, and the greatest attention. Many are the ways that are practised in cleaning it, by different servants, every one thinks his own way the best, and many times the plate is injured, by different servants, trying different experiments on it; but I shall give you, in the index of this book, two of the best recipes for making plate powder, that is used by one of the best silver smiths in London. Before you clean your plate with this powder, you must wash it well in a great hot suds, that there may be no grease left on it, for you never can clean plate in a proper manner if it is greasy. You may use either of these plate powders wet or dry. If your plate be very dirty I should recommend it wet. To mix it wet, take some of your powder and wet it with spirits of wine to the consistency of cream, then take a piece of fine soft sponge that is free from grit or dirt of any kind whatever, dip it in this mixture, then squeeze it a little so as you will not waste it, then apply it quick and even all over your plate; do not rub over too much at a time, as it ought to be polished before it gets too dry.

To polish your plate, you should have some soft linen rags or cloths to rub off the mixture, and then polish them off with your shammy leather. When you have dishes, salvers, salts, and other articles that are ornamented, that is, etched and beaded in rough ornamental work, you must have three good plate brushes; one must be hard as a tooth brush, and another something softer, and the third quite soft. The hard brush is for the rough work, and you must recollect never to brush any silver that is plain, with the hard brush, as you are sure to scratch it; the soft brushes are for the handles of your silver knives and forks, which generally want brushing.

CLEANING PLATE WITH DRY PLATE POWDER

This gives plate a most brilliant lustre, if it is only well done; and should be rubbed on with your naked hand, such as spoons, forks, and dessert knives that have silver blades. These small articles are cleaned by taking some of the powder between your finger and thumb, and the longer you rub, the better it will look; any article of your plate that is ornamented, this part may be rubbed with a piece of leather dipped in the plate powder, and rubbed quick and hard; then it should be brushed with your plate brushes, as in the other directions, and polished off with your shammy or wash leather; and I will warrant your plate to look beautiful.

In the next place you must remember to keep your plate in a dry place, for if you let any articles that are only plated, lay about dirty, or in a damp place, they are sure to rust if plated on steel; and if plated on copper, they are sure to canker; therefore you should be particular, and not leave salt or acids of any kind on plated ware, as it is sure to take off the plate, and leave a stain, and by rubbing this stain, the plate will rub off; by which means the article is perfectly spoiled. I very well know that there are many articles of this kind, that are often spoiled through the neglect of servants, and especially young hands, that have had no experience of those things; therefore, my young friends, I have here given you such directions as I trust will enable you to keep your plate in such order as may give general satisfaction to your employers, and gain credit for yourselves.

I shall point out to you the next part of your work, in the following pages.

———

CLEANING SILVER AND PLATED CANDLESTICKS

This is another branch of a house servant's business, which should command the greatest attention and neatness; as there is nothing that adds more to the reputation of a servant than to see his candlesticks and candles kept in good order. When you are about to clean your silver or plated candlesticks, you should be very careful that you do not scratch them, therefore the best method of cleaning them is to take some good hot and strong soap suds, have a piece of soft flannel, and immerse it in the water or suds, as hot as you can bear your hand in it; wash your candlesticks one at a time, taking great care not to wet the green baize, which is generally rosined to the foot of the candlesticks. When washed clean, have some soft towels for that purpose, and wipe them as quick as you wash them; when you have them all finished, take your shammy leather, with a little whiting dusted over them with your little muslin bag, which you must have filled with whiting, for this or other purposes.

When your candlesticks are most sublimely finished, then you must see to your candles. You should be very particular to keep your candles in a clean cool place, as there is nothing that looks worse, than candles taken into the parlour, when all over dust or smut. Be careful when putting up your candles into the candlesticks, that you do not break them. If they are too large for the sockets, scrape them down very neat and even, so as to fit; and should they be too small, take some paper, double it and let it be about an inch wide, wrap this around the end of your candle, so as to fit the socket, but don't let any of the paper appear above the candlestick.

DIRECTIONS FOR SETTING UP THE CANDLES

You should always make it a regular rule to set up your candles in the morning, and particularly your chamber candlesticks, as they are often called for in the course of the day, to seal letters, &c. The others should likewise be put up, and in order, for suppose they are called for in a hurry, and at a time when you cannot find leisure to get your candles and set them up? besides, when you are in a hurry and bustle, you are very apt to break them, and this causes great delay, and it looks very bad to see the company waiting so long, after they have been ordered, and it likewise puts yourself into a state of confusion, &c. Should you have wax candles for use, be careful and have your hands clean, or you will soil them. Before you set them up in candlesticks, you should rub them with a piece of soft paper, and dip the tops of the wick in spirits of wine; this will make them easy to light.

There are some servants that light the candles before they put them up; but I do not approve of this plan, for you cannot light them and blow them out again, without causing them to swale or drop down the sides, which makes them have a bad appearance. You should have some wax tapers on purpose to light your candles with, as paper makes a dirt, and flies about the room; besides it generally sticks to the candle and causes it to burn dim. If you have branches around your drawing room, and they are to be lit up when there is a party, you must trim your wax candles most sublimely, with some white paper cut in the form of a rose, to go round the end of the candles, and fit neatly round the socket of the branch; this looks very well at night. You should likewise have a piece of taper tied on the end of a piece of rattan, on purpose for lighting them, as it is very awkward to bring steps into the room.

CLEANING POLISHED STEEL GRATES

These, and polished steel fire irons, are things that require great care and attention to keep them bright and free from rust; I therefore shall give you some instructions how to keep them in good order. In the first place if the bright bars are very dirty and black, use the following mixture.

Take half a pound of soft soap. Put it into one quart of soft water and boil it down to a pint, then take some emery and mix in a portion of this liquid. Brush off all the soot and dirt from your grate, and take a piece of thick cloth and dip it into the mixture, then rub quick and hard, and in a few minutes you will get off all the black and dirt. After which take some crocus and wet it with N. E. rum, or gin, to the consistency of paint, with a piece of flannel dipped into it, and rub it quick and hard, until the bars, &c. become bright, then take some old pieces of linen or cotton, which you must have for this purpose, and rub all the mixture clean off. Then take a piece of leather and some dry rotten stone, and in a few minutes quick rubbing, you will have a beautiful polish. If your fire irons should happen to get rusty, as they often do in damp weather, and especially when there is no fire in the room, rub them well over with a piece of flannel dipt in sweet oil, then shake over them some fresh slacked lime, and let them lay for twenty four hours, or more if necessary, in this state, then take a piece of flannel and give them a good rubbing; when the lime and oil is clean off, then use the crocus and gin as above directed, and polish off as the grate. This is a most sublime method of polishing and cleaning all polished steel articles, &c.

DIRECTIONS FOR CLEANING MAHOGANY FURNITURE

Another branch of a house servant's business is to attend to cleaning the tables, sideboards, mahogany chairs, and the parlour doors, if mahogany; likewise mahogany trays and any other article of mahogany that is in the parlour or drawing room. You should pay a great deal of attention to cleaning furniture, to make it look well. If your furniture be of a dark colour, you should be very careful with what mixture you clean it; but you will find directions for light and dark, referred to in the Index. When you have cleaned off the dust from your furniture, and when you put on your oil, or paste, put but little on at a time, rubbing it well in, with a piece of flannel. You must put it on very even, and rub very quick, and in a short time you will have a beautiful and brilliant polish. If you should use oil, you must rub as quick as you possibly can, taking care to rub with the grain of the wood, with a piece of flannel; and when you have it well rubbed, take another piece of flannel and give it a good rubbing a second time, then polish off with some fine linen cloths or a silk handkerchief; the latter is very good to give it a good gloss. If you clean your tables with bees wax and spirits of turpentine mixed together, this is as good a thing as I could recommend; it's a thing that requires but little rubbing, and is better for furniture than any other mixture now in use; I shall therefore give you directions how to use this mixture. Take a piece of flannel and apply some of this mixture on it, then rub it quick and even all over your furniture, and in a short time you will have a most brilliant polish. Finish off with an old silk handkerchief. You will find directions for this receipt in the Index.

HINTS ON TAKING OUT
STAINS FROM MAHOGANY

There are some times that your tables will want washing; when there has been too much wax, oil, or paste put on, and not well rubbed off, the dust settles on it, and it is impossible for you to get them to look well, if this is not washed off with the following wash;—Take some warm beer, and a piece of flannel immersed into it; with this, wash off your tables, and recollect to rub them quick and even; after you have got your tables quite dry, then apply your mixture; take pains and rub it well in, as it will want much more of your mixture than when they were not washed, but they will look of a much brighter and more brilliant colour. You will find how to take out all your ink, and other stains, by the directions given in the receipts.

When you clean your chairs, remove them all out into the middle of the room. I have often seen, in many houses where I have been, the walls marked and smutted all over with the oil, or whatever they cleaned their furniture with. This has a very bad appearance; besides, it disfigures the walls in a ridiculous manner, and shows great neglect of neatness in the servant. Therefore, when you clean your chairs, sideboards, &c. always move them from the walls, and be very particular about the backs of your chairs, and the edges of the tables, that you do not leave any of your mixture, to dirty the ladies' or gentlemen's clothes, as this would be a sad affair. But I trust you will follow these remarks and observations which I have laid down, and you are sure to give general satisfaction.

BRUSHING AND FOLDING
GENTLEMEN'S CLOTHES

This is another part of a house servant's business, which requires a great deal of care, as good clothes are often spoiled through neglect and bad management. Therefore I shall endeavour to give you some directions and insight of brushing and folding them up in a proper manner. In the first place, if your gentleman's clothes should happen to get wet or muddy, hang them out in the sun or before the fire to dry. Do not attempt to brush them while wet, or you will surely spoil them, but as soon as they are perfectly dry, take and rub them between your hands where there are any spots of mud, then hang them on your clothes horse, which you must have for the purpose; then take a rattan and give them a whipping, to take out the dust, but be careful and don't hit the buttons, or you will be apt to break or scratch them.

When this is done, take your coat and spread it on a table at its full length. Let the collar be towards the left hand, and the brush in your right, then brush the back of the collar first, between the shoulders next, then the sleeves and cuffs, then brush the farthest lapel and skirt, then the near one, observing to brush with the nap of the cloth, as it runs towards the skirts. When all these parts are properly done, then fold as follows.— Double the off sleeve from the elbow towards the collar, the other the same way; then turn the lapel over the sleeve as far as the back seam, and the other in the same manner; then turn up the off skirt so that the end may touch the collar; the near one the same; give it a light brush over, and then turn one half the coat right even over the other, and you will find the coat folded in a manner that will gain you credit from any gentleman, and will keep smooth for any journey.

BRUSHING AND CLEANING GENTLEMEN'S HATS

This is another part of a gentleman's wardrobe, that you should pay much care and attention to, or otherwise it will soon look shabby. You should have a soft camels hair brush to brush your hats with, as this brush will not injure the fur, nor scratch it off. Should the hat happen to get wet, you must handle it as lightly as possible, or you will put it out of form, but to remedy this, you should put your left hand with your fingers extended open, into the hat, then take a silk handkerchief in your right hand and rub it lightly all round, the way the fur goes, until almost dry; then take your hat brush and brush it the way the fur goes until almost dry; if the fur sticks and does not brush smooth, you must take the brush that you polish your shoes with. Should the fur not come smooth, you must dip a sponge in some beer or spirits of wine, the latter is preferable, as it gives a brilliant jet lustre to the fur. Continue to brush with your hard brush until dry; then give it a light rub over with a silk handkerchief, and put in your hat stick. There are some people that think brushing a hat while it is wet, certainly spoils it; but it is quite the contrary; for the hatters themselves always brush and finish off their hats while damp, so as to give the fur a brilliant appearance. Likewise they set them to their regular shape while damp. I have received these instructions myself, from one of the best hat manufacturers in London; and I hope that my young friends will follow the example, that their mode of working may be a credit to themselves, and give general satisfaction to their employers; therefore I shall proceed to give you some instructions in the following pages, on the next part of your work.

REGULATIONS FOR THE PANTRY

The pantry is the place where the footman generally does the most part of his work, such as to clean his plate, trim his salts and casters, and trim his lamps and candlesticks, wash his breakfast things, and his glasses and silver after dinner, and several other articles; therefore you should be very particular in keeping it clean and neat, and have all your drawers and lockers for their several uses. Make it a general rule always to have every thing in its proper place, as nothing looks worse than to see every thing topsy turvy; this is an English phrase, but the meaning is, to see every thing in its wrong place; for the beauty of a good servant is to have a proper place for every thing that is used in common, that he may know where to lay his hand upon it, when it is wanted; this will be greatly to your advantage.

In the next place you must have a small tub to wash your breakfast things in, and another for your glasses, as the one you wash your breakfast things in generally is greasy, as you often have eggs, sausages, ham, &c. for breakfast. You should likewise have a sufficiency of towels, as it is impossible to do work without good materials to do it with, therefore you should have cloths for your glasses, tea things, and likewise for your knives, knife trays, and lamps, and always use your towels for their proper uses; your water for your tea things should be as hot as you can bear your hands in it. Put in a little soap, as it gives china a fine polish and keeps them from having a greasy feeling; do not put too many tea cups or saucers in at a time for fear of breaking them; be particular and wipe them very dry and clean, and put them by neat and tidy; there is nothing stands more high for the reputation of a servant, than to see his pantry kept neat, and every thing in it handsomely arranged in its place.

DIRECTIONS FOR CLEANING TEA TRAYS

This is another part of your work that requires much care, as such articles are often spoiled through not being properly attended to. In the first place you never should pour boiling water on a tray, as it makes the varnish crack and peel off. When your japan trays are dirty, take a sponge and dip it in warm water, rub on a little soap, and wash your tray with this; wipe it dry, and if it looks smeary, dust a little flour over it, and polish off with a dry cloth. This is the most safe and best way to clean and polish japanned tea trays. If your paper trays should get spotted, take a piece of flannel, dip it in some sweet oil, and rub it over the spots; if any thing can take them out, this will. Polish off with a soft cloth, then lightly with an old silk handkerchief, which you must keep for this purpose.

In the next place you must be very particular in wiping out your tea urn after it is emptied. Never leave any wet on the outside, for it will leave marks after it. Always make it a general rule to put away every thing in its proper place; and never leave your glasses, trays, or plate about dirty any longer than you can get a chance to wash them and put them away; for if they are left around, they are apt to get broken, and of course it will be laid to your negligence, which surely it is. There are many houses that you may go into and find the pantry in a sad dilemma, and at an hour of the day when a servant ought to be ashamed to have his things so disorderly. There is nothing that points out a good, capable servant, so soon as to see his things kept in good order, and in their proper places.

————

WASHING AND CLEANING DECANTERS

In washing decanters, the greatest care should be taken, both as to what you clean them with, and that you do not break them. There are various ways of cleaning them, and every one thinks his own way the best. There are some that recommend sand, cinders, coals, &c. and more above them, recommend sand-paper, egg-shells, wood-ashes, and what not. I have tried almost all these articles, but none of them have answered my expectations, for the whole of these articles have a kind of a scratching quality about them, very unfit for this purpose; therefore I shall give you directions for one that has fully answered my purpose for many years. In the first place, take some thick brown paper, cut it up into small pieces, then roll it between your hands, and put it into your decanter, with a few bits of soap cut small; then pour into the decanter some warm water, not boiling, and shake them about for some time, until you see the scum and dirt quite disappear. You may add in a little pearl ashes with the soap. Should any of the crust of the wine appear, apply a piece of sponge made fast to a piece of cane or strick for this purpose; this will remove all the scum or crust of the wine out of the old scratches, and give your decanters a beautiful polish. Rinse them twice in cold clean water, and turn up to drain; when they are well drained, wipe them clean with your glass towel, and afterwards take your shammy leather to give them the last polish. If they are cut glass, you must have a brush to brush the lint which your glass cloth may leave in the cutting, or rough work, then give them a good polish with your shammy leather, and put them away in their proper places. Now, my young friends, I have here given you instructions how to proceed, and I sincerely wish that you may follow the example.

ON TRIMMING THE CRUET
STAND OR CASTERS

This is the most particular article that belongs to your dinner utensils; therefore you should remember to examine it every day to see if all the cruets are clean, and full of every thing that is necessary to have in them, such as mustard, oil, vinegar, catsup, soy, black pepper, and cayenne, or other sauces that you may have bottles for; therefore you should always see that your casters are furnished with all those articles daily, as there is nothing that looks so negligent in a servant, than to want for any of these articles when called for by any of the company. Besides, it is a great mortification to your employers, as a lady should not want to be troubled to look after these things, if she has a man that is capable of his business. You should therefore make it your chief study to keep every thing in good order that is under your care and influence; it will not only gain credit from your employers, but meet the approbation of other ladies and gentlemen who may visit there. In the next place you should never leave your mustard spoon in your mustard after dinner is over, or your salt spoons in your salt cellars, especially if they are silver or plated, as salt left on any plated article is sure to rust or canker, therefore you should always wash your mustard and salt spoons, when you are washing up your glasses and silver, after dinner; and you should likewise empty out your salt, and wipe dry your salt cellars, and put them away in their proper places; you will find directions, by looking for them in the Index, for mixing your mustard and all other articles which you may have occasion for using. You should mix but little mustard at a time, as it is much better when fresh made. You should never waste any thing, for it is a very wicked thing to waste or destroy any of your employer's property, except what is absolutely necessary.

TO CLEAN TEA AND COFFEE URNS

These are articles that should be taken great care of, as they are generally very expensive, and if not taken care of, they are easily spoiled. If your tea or coffee urns are silver or plated, you must clean, as under the head of Plate; but if they are bronze, you must clean them as per direction in the Index. Be very particular when you put by your urns, that they are perfectly dry inside; if not they are apt to get musty. Should you put by your urns to remain any length of time, take and fill them with old paper; it is a very good plan to have covers made for your urns, as this prevents flies from dirtying them, and likewise keeps them free from dust or damp. You should be very careful when you are filling your urn, that the water or coffee is on a level with the heater, if not the heater is very apt to burn the sides and top of the urn.

You must likewise be very careful when you put in your heater, that you do not let it down too heavy, as there is great danger of breaking the bottom of the urn. Tea and coffee urns are often spoiled through servants not studying such observations as these. There should be a proper hook to put in the heater and to take it out, and by this way you will never injure your urn. In the next place you must always have your water that is for tea, boiling, before you put it into the urn, for it is impossible to make good tea if the water does not boil, even if the tea is of ever so good a quality. Now, my young friends, I have here given you instructions concerning your tea and coffee urns, and how to manage them; therefore I trust that you will imitate them as near as possible, and always study to give general satisfaction to those you serve.

MAHOGANY DINNER TRAYS

These are another part of your work, that should be kept in good order, as they are a part of the furniture, which is most commonly carried in and out of the parlour, through the course of dinner; therefore you should endeavour to keep them clean and in good order, as they are exposed to the eyes of the company. You should clean them as the rest of the mahogany, but you will often have to wash them, as they are liable to have gravy and other sauces spilled in them, during the carrying up and down of the dinner; but as soon as dinner is over, you should wash out your trays if they want it, and hang them up in their proper places, until you clean them the next day, when you are cleaning your furniture.

There is nothing so advantageous to a servant as to have good rules to work by, therefore his principal one should be, to keep every thing in its proper place, and in good order. I have lived in families where I could go to my pantry at any hour of the night, let it be ever so dark, and lay my hand on any thing that I wanted, as quick and with as little noise as if I had a light. This is easily done, if you only give yourself the habit of putting things by tidy and in their proper places. Should you have a sink in your pantry, as there generally is, be very particular in keeping it clean; throw no tea leaves or any dirt that may stop up the waste pipe; if you do, the water will grow stagnated, and cause a bad smell, which is very disagreeable. After you have done washing up your glasses, rinse out your sink with clean water, wipe it dry with a coarse towel, that you must have for that purpose.

REMARKS ON THE MORNING'S WORK IN WINTER TIME

Now, my young friends, I shall here give you some instructions how to proceed with your morning's work, in winter time. In the first place, make it your business to have plenty of wood, coal, or whatever fuel you burn, in its proper place over night, as it will save you a great deal of time in the morning, as the mornings are so short at this season of the year, and it is a great advantage to have these necessaries in readiness, where perhaps you have three or four fires to make, and grates and fire irons to clean before the family rises. In the next place you should rise early so as to be able to have your fires made and the rooms warm before you clean yourself for breakfast. Therefore, when you first come down, make as little noise as you possibly can in opening your rooms where you have fires to make, then proceed to take up your ashes, clean your grates, or fire irons, and tidy up your hearth. When this is done, proceed to make your fires. When they are all made, and burning well, then wash your hands, and open your shutters, and proceed to set out your breakfast table. When this is done, go round and see that all your fires burn well, or if they want replenishing, that the rooms may be warm and comfortable against your family come down stairs. Keep all your doors shut, and then, if you think you have time to clean your front-door brasses before they come down, it is a very desirable job to get out of the way before the family come down; but you can judge as to what time you have to spare. As you should have yourself clean and tidy against they come down to breakfast, you should always clean your boots and shoes over night, because it gives you more time in the morning.

DIRECTIONS FOR SETTING OUT THE BREAKFAST TABLE

Now, my young friends, I shall give you some instructions how to set out your breakfast, dinner, and tea tables; but I first will give you instructions for your breakfast table. In the first place, say all your things are clean and in readiness in your pantry, as they should be, and that your family for breakfast consists of six or eight people. In the first place, dust off your table clean, and spread your cloth neatly, observing that the centre crease of your cloth is right in the centre of the table, and that it don't hang longer at one end than at the other; then proceed to set out your breakfast tray; laying a cup and saucer for each person, with a teaspoon in each saucer, at the right hand side of the cup; then set in the centre of the tray, your sugar pot on the right hand, your cream pot on the left, and your slop bowl in the centre, with your tea pot behind them, so as to be right under the tea urn, and that the tap of the urn may reach it, when on the table. As soon as you have this done, set your tray at the end of the table where the lady sits that pours out the tea, then put around your plates, one for each person, putting them at a proper distance from each other; then your knife and fork to each small plate, the knife on the right hand, the fork on the left, with the end of the handles even with the edge of the table; you must always have salt on the table, as most families have eggs, or some kinds of meat on the table for breakfast.

In summer, you must put your butter and cream to cool some time before you have set your table. If you have not a proper cooler, take a large bowl, and half fill it with water, then put a small plate in the bottom of the bowl, then put in your butter and cream pot, then a small piece of ice, if you use any. This is a very good method to cool your butter and cream for breakfast. If your breakfast table is rather small you must spread a napkin on a small stand, place it on the left hand side of the lady that makes tea; place on this the tea caddy, and if there is not room on the breakfast tray, for all your cups and saucers to be placed uniform, you may put the remainder on the stand. Remember to put on a knife for your bread and one for the butter, and if any cold meat is put on the table lay a dinner knife and fork to it for carving; and if there are eggs, do not forget the spoons; and if you don't use egg cups and stands, you must put on wine glasses. If any of your family like mustard with their meat, you must put the cruet stand or casters on the stand.

When you have every thing properly arranged on your breakfast table, then put round the chairs, and if it is cold weather, see that your fires burn well, and your room comfortable, against the family come down to breakfast; then see that the water boils, and that your heater is in good order for your urn. Always fill your urn before you put in your heater; and don't forget your urn ring if they use one.

When you take in the urn, place it exactly behind the tea pot, that the tap may come over it, and be near enough to the person that makes tea, that they may turn it into the tea pot without standing up.

Whatever you have to carry in for breakfast, such as toast, rolls, eggs, &c. always take them in on a waiter; never carry in, or hand any thing with the naked hand, as it looks very ungenteel. Now I have given you full instructions for your breakfast table, I shall proceed to give you instructions for your dinner table.

REGULATIONS FOR THE DINNER TABLE

There is not any part of a servant's business that requires greater attention and systematical neatness, than setting out his dinner table, and managing for a party of sixteen or eighteen people. It is a branch of a servant's business wherein he can show more of his ability than in any thing else that he may have to encounter. There are many servants, we very well know, that make great pretensions to conducting a party or dinner, who yet never knew the first principles of properly waiting at table. This causes great confusion in a house, both to the family, and the rest of the servants. It is no easy thing to be able to wait properly at dinner, and to have every thing done in proper and systematical order. I am very sorry to say, that I have seldom met with many servants who could properly manage a dinner party of sixteen or eighteen, without confusion in some part or the other of it; and particularly in small families, where they have company but seldom. Confusion often occurs, through not having a sufficiency of things for the party, without having to wash plates, spoons, &c. while at dinner; and it likewise too often happens, through fault of the servant at the head of the family not knowing his business.

In the first place, the greatest attention should be paid, to have all the things that are for use properly arranged, and appointing each attendant his proper place, and what he has to do. You will always find that the more help there is to wait on table, the more confusion there is, especially if their different offices are not pointed out before dinner by the servant that is to conduct the dinner. I have always found that one good servant that understands his business, can do more work in its proper order than three awkward ones, as they are chiefly in each other's way, and this causes a great confusion in the course of dinner. There are some families that think a servant ought to wait on eight or ten at dinner, but I tell them they are much mistaken; for this is too many for one man to wait upon, to do it to perfection; and especially if there are many changes. Therefore, my young friends, I have now brought you thus far; and given you general directions in the various branches before laid down, in which I have generally addressed myself to all; I therefore shall now address myself to Joseph personally, and consider him as having a party of ten, where there is no man servant kept but himself, and no one to show him but himself, and where he must be answerable for conducting the party alone; therefore I shall give him all the instructions in my power; and by the rest of my young friends listening with attention, it may prepare them for such situations in future.

Now, Joseph, the first thing that is to be attended to, is to enquire of the cook what there is for dinner; by doing this you will be able to judge what things you may want, as it is a very awkward thing to leave the room, in the middle of the dinner, for things that you should have had before the dinner was served up. In the next place you should ask the cook if there is any particular way of sending things up; as you may make sad mistakes if you have not a bill of fare, and should you have one, you will not be at a loss how to put the dinner on the table in proper order, as it is there directed.

LAYING THE CLOTH, &C.

In putting the cloth on the table, you should be very particular, observing, in the first place, to have its right side uppermost. This you may easily learn by looking at the hem and fold. Likewise you must be very particular to have the bottom of the cloth to the bottom of the table. In most all dinner cloths that are spread for company, there is generally some ornamental work wrought on them, on some there is the family's coat de arms, on others, baskets of flowers, birds, branches, &c. Then suppose there is a basket of flowers, the bottom of the basket should be towards the person at the bottom of the table, as the design should always go up the table; the centre of the table cloth should likewise go exactly down the centre of the table, and not hang the eighth of an inch longer at one end than the other.

SETTING OUT THE DINNER TABLE

When your cloth is perfectly even, then put round your plates, laying four at each side, and one at each end, observing to have them at equal distance from each other, then put on your napkins, having them neatly folded so as to admit the bread into them, without being seen; then put round your knives and forks, placing the knives at the right hand, with the edge of the blade towards the plate, and the end of the handle to come even with the edge of the table; then place round your forks, on the left hand, in the same manner; then put your carving knife and fork head and point, in the same way. When you have this done, put a dinner knife and fork at each side of the table, opposite the centre, for carving with; then put round your tumblers, one at the right side of each plate, about three inches from the edge of the table. The best method to have them at an equal distance from the edge of the table is, to take a steel fork, hold the prong in your right hand, allowing about three inches of the handle and prong to be extended from your fore finger and thumb, then press your fore finger against the edge of the table, letting the handle of the fork go in on the table; then draw your tumbler so as to touch the handle of the fork; and so on to each tumbler. By this process you will be able to have our tumblers at a proper distance from the edge of the table; then put round your wine glasses, one before each tumbler; and this will keep them even, in like manner; then put round your plates; put a spoon between each plate in a straight line all around the table, with the bowls upwards, as they show much better to advantage; then put on your two large gravy spoons, one at the bottom, and another at the top. Put these across, before the head and foot plate; then put round your salts, which should be six in number, as this is the regular quantity for ten to dinner. Remember to put on your salt spoons, and if you have a sallad to go in the centre of the table, lay a silver waiter under it, so as to raise your sallad bowl more majestically. If you have four wines, put one at each corner of the table, but not so near as to be knocked off. When removing the dishes, if your family dine by candle light, the candlesticks or branches are put in the centre of the table. Should there be branches, the sallad or epergne must be put in the centre, with one of the branches between that and the bottom, and the other between that and the top; you should have plenty of plates, knives and forks, spoons, glasses of both kinds, and every thing else that is necessary for your dinner; as it is much better to have in the

room more things than are wanted, of every description, than not
to have enough; as this causes great confusion.

SETTING OUT THE SIDEBOARD

In setting out your sideboard, you must study neatness, convenience, and taste; as you must think that ladies and gentlemen
that have splendid and costly articles, wish to have them seen and
set out to the best advantage. I have often seen at parties, where
I have been attending, side boards and side tables set out in such
a manner that they looked quite in a state of confusion; whereas,
if they were set out in a proper order, they would make a magnif-
icent appearance. There are some old and experienced servants,
that will set out their tables and side boards with such a degree of
taste and neatness, that they will strike the eyes of every person
who enters the room, with a pleasing sensation of elegance.

The grapes which are to go on with the dessert, &c. with all
the spare glasses that are for dinner, must go on the sideboard,
with your champaign, hawk, and ale glasses. When all these are
properly arranged, they make a grand display. Your glasses
should form a crescent, or half circle, as this looks most sublime.
If you should have a light on your sideboard, you must leave a
vacant place behind your glasses for it; in forming the crescent,
your highest glasses must be the farthest off, and the smaller
ones in an inner circle. Let them be put two and two, that is, one
large and one small, that you may have them ready when
wanted. In the space between the glasses, place your cruet-
stand or casters, this must be right in the centre of the sideboard, and about two inches from the edge; then put at each
side of your casters your two water decanters, then your small
silver hand waiters, one on each side of each water decanter,
then your wine for the dessert, in the silver coursters, in the
same manner; then if there is any vacancy left, you may fill it up
with some spoons, as spoons, &c. give glass a brilliant display. If
your sideboard is very large, you may put your finger glasses on
it, but mind that every thing looks uniform. In the next place,
put your plate basket in the most convenient place, with your
knife trays and clean cloths spread in them. Keep one of them

for removing the knives from the dishes, before you take the dishes from the table.

You never should take a dish from the table with the knife and fork in it, as it is very dangerous; if the knife or fork should fall off, it might perhaps stick in your foot, or, on the other hand, it will dirty the carpet, which is a very disagreeable thing, and is sure to give dissatisfaction to the lady of the family.

There are many such disasters as this that happen through the servant's not attending properly to the regular rules of waiting at table. There are many servants that put themselves quite in a state of confusion, by being in too great a hurry. The beauty of a servant is to go quietly about the room when changing plates or dishes; he never should seem to be in the least hurry or confusion, for this plainly shows that he is deficient of his duty. A man that knows his business well, should take hold of things as a first rate mechanic, and never seem to be agitated in the least. You should always have a quick, but light and smooth step, around the room while waiting; practice will soon bring you to this. And in the next place you should always wear tight shoes or thin pumps while waiting at dinner, as it is impossible for you to go quick and light, if you wear heavy shoes or boots, in the parlour.

THE SIDE TABLE

The side table is the place where you are to have all your dinner plates, pudding and cheese plates, and likewise the dessert plates, if there is not room on your sideboard for them. You must have a clean cloth spread upon it, as your salad and cold meats are to be placed on it, if they are not put on your dinner table. Divide your dinner plates into three piles; place one pile in the centre of the side table, about two inches from the edge, then place your other two piles, one on each side, leaving a regular space between them, so as to place your knives and forks between them, and this you must do with great taste, that they may look ornamental like the things on your sideboard, observing the same rule, to have every thing that is wanted first, next at hand. Place in the space that is left between the centre pile and that on the right hand, your large knives and forks, letting the ends of all the handles be on an even line with the edge of the table; then in the space on the left of the centre pile, set your small knives and forks, in the same manner, observing every thing to be uniform and in its proper place. Then place a pile of your small cheese plates behind the pile of large ones at the left of the centre, and your pudding plates behind the pile on the right, having each pile of an even height. But there should be no more than a dozen and a half in each pile, at most. Should there be any more vacant places, ornament them with some spoons, and your sauce ladles; having the bowls uppermost, as they show to more advantage; but leave room enough behind for your cold meats, if there is any; then put your dowlases on your dessert plates, with a dessert knife, fork and spoon, the knife to the right side and the fork to the left, with the spoon in the centre. Place those neatly on your side table, if there is not room on the sideboard for them; but the sideboard is the proper place, as they are convenient to the dessert glasses, &c.

In setting out your sideboard and sidetable you should always study convenience and elegance, in putting your things on, and study to have plenty of every thing, that you need not have to leave the room during the course of dinner. You must never be afraid of a little trouble when there is company, for where the sideboard and sidetable is set out with taste and ingenuity, it has a very pleasing effect to those who go in and see order and design prevail.

Never bring in your cheese before wanted, as the smell may be disagreeable to some of the company.

In the next place you should be careful not to make any more noise than you possibly can. When changing the plates, take off your dirty knife and fork very gently, and lay them in your knife tray, and put the plate into the plate basket as gently as you can. When returning a clean plate, lay your knife and fork on it as easy as you can, so as to cause no rattle or noise. Put the knife on the right and the fork on the left in the bowl of the plate, and lay it before the lady or gentleman as gently as possible. Always observe to go to the left side of the person that you hand any thing to, or take any thing from, as it is very awkward to hand any thing at the right hand side of the person; I have seen many accidents happen through the neglect of not practising these rules. In many cases there have been

whole glasses of beer, water, and wine, upset, all through handing it at the right hand side; for instance, perhaps the gentleman to whom you are taking the glass of beer, &c. may raise
his arm, and thus upset the whole.

DINNER ON THE TABLE

When your dinner is on the table, and every thing that is necessary, stand at the bottom and cast your eyes along the table,
and you will perceive in an instant if any of your dishes are not
properly placed. You should observe to have your side dishes in
a straight line, and at a regular distance from each other, and
also match in size and colour, cross corners, your four corner
dishes should go rather on a square, and to match each other
cross corner; as a middling dinner when well served up, and the
dishes well matched, and at a proper distance from each other,
has a more pleasing aspect than double as large a one, when
crowded, and improperly put on table; you should pay the greatest attention to this rule.

WAITING ON DINNER

When the chairs are put round, and all things quite ready,
proceed to the drawing room, or wherever the company is. If
the drawing room is large, advance a little towards the lady or
gentleman of the family, and with a graceful motion of your
head, say, "Ma'am," or "Sir, the dinner is served;" or "Ladies and
Gentlemen, dinner is on the table." When you see that they
have noticed the announcement, then proceed to the dining
room door, and hold it open until the company have all gone in,
then shut it, and when the company have sat down, if there is
soup, take off the cover; if there should be only fish at the top,
and a joint at the bottom, remove the cover from off the fish or
soup, and from off the proper sauce for the fish; and if there is
no one but yourself to wait, take your station at the bottom of
the table, about a yard behind the person that sits at the foot of
the table; stand rather a little to the left of his chair. By standing
in this position, you will command a full view of the table;
whereas if you stand behind the person that carves, at the bottom of the table, you cannot see when the plates want changing.

When you hold a plate to the carver to help a lady or gentleman, stand at the left hand of the carver, holding the plate in your left hand, with your thumb on the rim of the plate, and your two fingers extended under the bottom; you should never let your thumb go farther than the rim of the plate, for it is a very improper thing to run your thumb half way across the plate. If you want to tip the dish for gravy, change the plate into your right hand, and be careful that you do not spill the gravy on the cloth. When you take it to whom it is for, go to the left side, and with your right hand take the plate that is done with, and with your left hand lay the other gently before them.

You should never lay a plate before a lady or gentleman at their right hand side, except by some particular reason, that you have to sit it down with your right hand on the right side. When you are holding a plate to a carver, or handing the vegetables or sauces round, you must hold them in your left hand at the left side of the person you have to serve; and keep your fingers extended under the bottom, and in the same manner as you hold a plate.

When you are taking off all your covers, begin at the bottom dish first, at the left hand side, taking them off with your left hand all round, until you come to the bottom again, then place them in your dinner tray until you have time to take or send them out of the room. When beer, cider, or water is called for, go to the right side as the tumbler stands on that side; and be careful that you do not run them over, as you will wet the cloth. When you hand a glass or any thing on a hand waiter, always go to the left side.

When you hand a glass, knife and fork, or any thing else to any of the company, always take a hand waiter, as it is very improper to hand any thing with the naked hand; likewise when you are taking any thing off the table, such as a glass, spoons, or any other small article, have a waiter in your left hand, and take off the article with your right. In the next place when you are ready for the removes, for the soup, and fish, ring the bell, that the cook may have it in readiness against you want it; but, before you remove the soups or fish, take your knife tray, and remove the soup ladle and fish knife from them, holding your knife tray in your left hand, and removing them with your right. As soon as the removes are put on the table, uncover them, taking care that you don't dirt the cloth with the drops of steam from the covers, but, to hinder this, turn up the covers quick.

Then the next thing is to exert your skill and ability, until the company is all served round, with meat, vegetables, &c. Then take your station, and keep your eyes and ears open, to see and hear what the company may want, or ask for. Do not wait to be asked for every thing by the company; for if you keep a sharp eye on the table, you will see many things wanted by persons who, perhaps, through being a little bashful, will not ask for themselves; such as bread, vegetables, or sauce; likewise what may be wanted on particular occasions, such as mustard to duck and goose, fish-sauce to fish, mint-sauce to lamb, lemon to veal, bread-sauce to fowls, &c. &c. When you remove or take off the dishes, if large, put your two hands to them; stand at the left side of the person who sits opposite; the small ones you may take off with your one hand, but you must be very careful that you do not spill the gravy on the cloth. Always take a firm hold of the dishes when taking them off the table; observing to keep your right hand up one side of the dish towards the centre of the table, and the left hand near the other end, keeping a firm grasp with your thumbs, and your fingers well extended under the dish; always lift the dishes high enough to clear the glasses, &c. &c.

When you perceive the company do not seem to eat of the dishes on the table, keep your eye on the lady or gentleman of the family, as they generally give the signal to remove the first course. You must give the cook information before dinner that you will ring the bell twice, as a signal for second course to be got ready. When you are taking off your dishes, do it very gently, but quick and handy. You must not seem to be in the least confusion, for there is nothing that looks so bad as to see a man in a bustle, or confused state, when he has the management of a party. He should always take hold of his work as if he understood it, and never seem to be agitated in the least.

As soon as you perceive the signal to remove the first course, take your knife-tray and remove all the knives, forks, and spoons, from all the dishes, and the ladles from out the sauce-boats, before you attempt to remove any of the dishes from off the table; when you have finished this part, then go to the bottom of the table, and begin at the bottom dish, on the left side, taking all before you as you go along, observing to keep on the left side of the person who sits opposite the dish you are taking; putting your two hands to the large ones as directed; and only your left hand to the small ones; and so on, all round the table, until you come to the bottom again.

Then proceed for your second course, which you may bring in on your dinner tray, if your tray is large enough. Place your second course into it as it is to go on the table, but if you have a bill of fare, you need not be so particular. Have your bill of fare in your tray, that you may make no mistakes, when putting your dishes on the table. Begin in the same manner as you took the others off, first at the bottom, then the left side, and so on all round, observing to place your dishes at a regular distance from each other. When you have them all put on in proper order, take off all the covers as you did the first course, beginning at the bottom, up the left side, taking them off with your left hand, and so on until you come to the bottom again. See that there are knives, forks, and spoons, to the dishes that want them; then be ready to wait on the company.

When you see that they are finished with the second course, then put round your small cheese plates as you take your others off, with a small knife; if there is salad, you must put on a fork likewise. Have your salad, butter, cheese, and cucumbers ready against the second course comes off; but there are many families that have the salad, butter, cheese, radishes, &c. all put on with the second course; this saves a great deal of trouble and waiting on. But if your family should like the other way best, when your second course is done with, take your knife-tray, and remove all the knives, forks, and spoons, from off the dishes. When this is done, take off all the dishes as directed in the other courses; then put on your cheese, &c. If there should be two cheeses, with butter, salad, cucumbers, radishes, &c. put your cheese at top and bottom, your salad in the centre, and your butter and radishes at the sides, two plates of butter, and two of radishes to be put cross corners, will make your table look much better than with one of each. When you have put a knife to your cheese, another to your butter, with your salad spoon to your salads, &c. then proceed to hand round the cheese and wait on the company. Sometimes there is champaign, porter, or ale handed round, while at cheese; but in other families, while at the second course; and in others when the dessert is put on the table; but the gentleman of the family most commonly gives directions about his wines, and when they are to be put on the table.

As soon as the company are done with the cheese, &c. take your knife-tray and remove your salad spoon, butter and cheese knife, then begin and take off the dishes, as you did in the other courses; then clear off all your dirty glasses. The best means of doing this is to have a large waiter; let one of those who help you, take a firm hold of it between his two hands, while you begin at the bottom of the table on the left side, and clear every glass, spoon, and knife away, while he is to follow you around with the waiter. When all is cleared away and the wine taken off the table, then take a large plate and a fork in your right hand, and take up all the pieces of bread, from the cloth; then take another plate and your table brush, or a clean towel rolled up, begin at the bottom on the left side, brushing off clean all the crumbs, until you come to the bottom again, then put round your finger glasses, one to each person, beginning at the bottom and going all round; you may put on those to the right side of the ladies or gentlemen. When the company are all done with their glasses, begin at the bottom and take them off all round. When this is done, take off your table cloth, napkins, &c. then take a towel and wipe off your table, beginning at the bottom, and wiping all round; then proceed to put round your plates.

PUTTING ON THE DESSERT

Put round your dessert plates one before each person, then your wine glasses, placing two on the right side of each plate, then put on your wine coursters, or decanter stands and wine; if only two, put one near the corner, top and bottom, on the right side. If four, one to each corner. If different wines, place them so as to match cross corners; recollect to observe the same rule in putting on the dessert as the other courses, unless you have more dishes in number, in this case you may put on the dishes, top, middle and bottom; before you put on the sides, if you have a cake, put it right in the centre, with your sugar basin and cut-glass water pitcher between the top and bottom dishes, in a right line down the centre of the table. Then put round your side dishes, beginning at the bottom on the left side, observing to keep them at equal distance from each other, and all your dishes to match in colour and size as near as possible, as this is the beauty of putting on your dessert. When you have all your dishes on the table, put a knife to your cake, and half a dozen of large spoons reverse to each other, down the centre of the table, to serve the dessert with. Should there be blancmange or ice creams, lay a small pile of plates, top and bottom; when there is ice creams, you must stop to serve it round to the company, until all are helped, then proceed to take all the dirty things out of the room, with as little noise as possible; let your clean things on the sideboard and sidetable remain until you clear away, after the company has retired from the room. Never seem to be in a hurry or bustle in leaving the room. When all your dirty things are cleared out, shut the door after you very gently, as you should never make more noise in the parlour than you can possibly help.

PREPARATIONS FOR TEA AND COFFEE

If your family do not dine by candle-light, perhaps, against dinner is over, it may be time to light your lamps in the hall, and on the staircase; likewise have all your lamps, branches, &c. in readiness in the drawing room, if not lighted, as the ladies never stop long in the dining room after the dessert is over. When all your lamps are lit, and every thing in order, see that your boiler is full and in readiness for tea, then see to your silver, and knives and forks, that they are all washed, wiped, and put away in their places, that they may be in readiness to clean in the morning; observe to put your silver forks and spoons in separate places, for if you put your forks and spoons together, they are apt to get scratched. You should likewise count your silver after it is washed up, for fear there should be any mislaid.

Then see to your glasses, wash and wipe them dry, then put them by in their proper places; tidy up your pantry, and by this means you will have room for your other dirty glasses, &c. that are used for the dessert. When the gentlemen have retired from the dining room, then go in and first put away all the chairs in their places, then put away the fruit, &c. in their place, then take a large tray and take all the glasses off. Put by the wine, and empty all your dessert plates, and carry all the dirty things out to your pantry, or where you may wash them up. Wipe off the table, and take out all the clean things that remain on the sideboard and side table. When all is cleared away, and your room put in order, then proceed to wash up your glasses and dessert plates, spoons, &c. Wipe dry and put every thing away in their proper places, hang your towels to dry, and have yourself in readiness against they order tea or coffee.

CARRYING TEA AND COFFEE AROUND

In some houses the drawing room is up stairs; should this be the case where you live, you must be very careful when carrying your tea and coffee up stairs, that you do not slop it over into the saucers, as this would have a slovenly appearance to the company. Your tray should be large, if there is much company, that the ladies may take their cup and saucer with ease. At the first round you should have one cup of tea between every two of coffee, as they generally take more coffee than tea at the first round. When placing your cups and saucers on the tray, be particular and have them all uniform and not crowded; with your sugar and cream in the centre, and the sugar tongs and handle of the cream pot towards the company. Have, on another tray, your cake, wafers, toast, bread and butter, &c. all neatly arranged to take round after you have served tea and coffee to all the company. But if you have a large party, you should have some person to hand round the cake, &c. at the same time that you are serving round tea.

When you first enter the room with the tea, cast your eyes around the company to observe where the most elderly lady is seated, then proceed forward and help her first, observing to lower the waiter, that the ladies may take their tea off with ease. When the ladies are all served, then proceed to help the gentlemen, beginning as with the ladies. When all the company are served with the first round, carry out your tray, and wipe it clean if wet, then take another waiter to receive the cups as soon as the ladies and gentlemen are done with them. During this interval, hand round your cake, &c. When you have received all your empty cups, rinse them out, and proceed to serve round another course, as before, beginning at the same lady, and going all round, leaving the lady of the family to be the last lady that is served, as the strangers must always be served first. This second round is generally enough, but hand round the cake, &c. once or twice after, then carry all out of the room, and, if cold weather, see that all your fires burn well.

OBSERVATIONS ON SUPPER, &c.

Now, my young friends, in the next place I shall give you some observations on the management of a supper party. In the first place, we will consider the party to be from twenty to thirty. Such parties are very common in private families of fashionable standing. In such parties they generally play at cards, &c.; therefore have your lamps or candles in good order and lighted up before the company has come, and, if cold weather, have your fires in good order; likewise have your card tables placed out, and your chairs adjusted, and every thing properly arranged and in uniform array, that every thing may go on in good order, and without any bustle whatever, that you may gain credit from your employers and the company likewise.

In the next place see that your tea and coffee things are in order, and all placed on your waiter in readiness, should they have tea or coffee, as they generally do, before supper; likewise have your glasses wiped and placed on your proper waiters, as there are generally refreshments carried up to the drawing room to the company before supper. Let every thing be in good order and in readiness, that there need be no confusion whatever. When you have every thing properly arranged, and your rooms comfortable, then tidy yourself up, so as to look smart and clean, and have yourself in readiness to wait on the company, and show them to the drawing room.

In some families the servant has to announce the several names of the company as they come, before entering the drawing-room. This is troublesome where there is not sufficient help kept; but it is a most fashionable thing in all families of distinc-

tion in England and France, that the lady and gentleman of the
family may receive them as they enter the drawing room, and
introduce them to the rest of the company.

OBSERVATIONS ON THE SUPPER TABLE

You should always lay your cloth for supper before the company comes, if you possibly can, as it saves you a great deal of
time which you may want afterwards, as the company generally
wish some refreshments carried up to them before supper, &c.
Likewise you should learn from the lady of the family how many
visitants are expected; this will be a guide to let you see what
length your table should be. When laying your cloth you must
be as particular as at dinner; let your knives, forks, spoons, and
salts be placed with the same uniformity as at dinner, with a
tumbler, wine glass, and if there is champaign, put on a glass
likewise to each plate; place your tumbler glasses the same distance as directed at dinner, with your wine glass and champaign
glass about one inch from your tumbler, but on a straight line;
let your champaign glass be behind your wine glass.

Coolers or finger glasses are seldom used at supper parties;
you must have four or six water decanters or cut glass pitchers,
on your supper table, as the company generally help themselves
at supper without the formality of more attendance than is necessary for comfort. If it is a cold supper, your plates may be all
cold; but if in cold weather, and some hot dishes, your plates
must be warm. And keep good fires, that the company may be
all comfortable. You may place all your cold dishes on as soon as
your table is laid, that you may have more leisure to place them
on in proper uniform and neatness. Have all your dishes to
match in size to each other on opposite sides if possible, and all
at proper and equal distance from each other. Should you not
have a bill of fare to go by, place them on in the best style you
possibly can, so that the dishes match each other in colours, &c.
cross corners. Have plenty of clean things in the room, and
know that every thing that you may want is in the room before
the company sits down. There is seldom much change of dishes
at a supper party, and especially if cold; for then it all goes on at
once; therefore you will not want as many clean articles of each

kind as at dinner, such as knives, forks, spoons, plates, &c. but have plenty of brimmer glasses, tumblers, and wine glasses, on your sideboard and to be set out as at dinner. Your wine decanters must be put on at supper, as at dinner. Make it your study to put every thing on with taste, and as though you had a design for taste and ingenuity. Supper dishes are generally, and ought always to be, garnished with green parsley or flowers; if they are, be very careful not to shake them off when going up stairs, as they give a supper table a most sublime appearance, and particularly in summer time, when every thing is green and in bloom.

In waiting at supper, you must observe the same rules as what I have given for dinner, and regulate according to the number that you are to have to assist you to wait, that there may not be the least bustle or confusion in waiting on the company, as this is one of the most disagreeable things that the lady or gentleman of the family can see; let each know his proper place appointed, and what he has to do; therefore if you abide by those rules, every thing will go on in good order, and without any confusion or mismanagement.

What can be more agreeable to the lady who gives the entertainment, than to see every thing go on with order and correctness, without having any blunders whatever; but, the company to be comfortably and systematically waited on; this will give general satisfaction to the family, and gain credit for yourself. As soon as supper is over and the company withdrawn from the supper table; then see to collecting your plate, and clearing your dirty things away, and put your clean things in their places.

DIRECTIONS FOR EXTINGUISHING THE LAMPS, SHUTTING UP THE HOUSE, &c.

As soon as you have all the clean articles put by in their proper places, and your room put to rights, then proceed to gather up your plate, &c. It is oftentimes that spoons, forks, &c. are thrown into the swill tub after a party, as the servants are generally in a bustle or hurry; so the present time is the best to count over your spoons, forks, &c. that if any are missing, you can make search immediately. In the next place, when the party has broken up, and all dispersed, proceed to extinguish your lamps, &c. Your lamps must be turned down, not blown out. Then put up the keys of your lamps, that the oil may not flow over, to spoil the carpets, for this would be a sad disaster; and it oftentimes happens through the neglect of servants not attending properly to the lamps. When all your lights are extinguished, see that your fireguards are put to your fires, and that every thing is safe in the rooms before you go out; then fasten your front door; then go round to all the doors and windows on the back part of the house, to ascertain whether they are all safe fastened. This is the most important part of a servant's duty, to see that the house, and all the fires are safe. It is so great and important a part of your duty, that the lives and property of your employers depend on it. How many instances have we heard and seen, of houses being burnt through the neglect of the servants not having paid proper attention to the fires and lights? and on the other hand how many houses have we heard of being robbed, through the neglect of the servant not paying proper attention to shutting the doors and fastening the windows? Another thing, you should have your hall door fastened at dusk, to prevent any one from coming in and stealing coats, cloaks, hats, &c. as this very often is the case in a city, and owing to the servants not fastening it in proper season.

Now, my young friends, I think that I have given you sufficient instruction, and a full and clear insight into the manner and ways of setting out tables, &c. and waiting on parties in a systematical and proper order, which I trust, from my own experience, is sure to give general satisfaction to your employers, to gain their approbation, and to get credit for yourself. Perhaps you may find some trifling difference in some families, in little ways and notions of their own, for almost every different family has some different rules of its own, and of course you are bound to comply with them, as soon as you enter under an engagement to serve with the family; for it is the duty of every servant to comply with his employer's wishes, and conform to his rules, even if he knows them to be imperfect. But still, the rules and observations which I have given, will be a true guide to those who may study and practise them, in the families whom they have the honour to serve.

They are all my own experience, for several years past, in some of the first families in England, France, and in the United States of America; and I am highly flattered that a work of this kind will be a most essential article to all private families; and likewise to those domestics that are not perfect, or properly taught the duty of a domestic, or house servant. There are many families that have the misfortune of meeting with men of this sort; and I am very well aware of the trouble that the lady of the family has with them, to bring them to understand their business, and by only having one of these books in the house for the use of the servant, they will be saved all that trouble, with only the exception of informing them of the rules of the family. I know there are many house servants that think themselves perfect in every branch of their duty; but, when coming to peruse this work, may find things that they are quite deficient in, and will see they never had the experience or opportunity of knowing. I sincerely hope that this work may do the same good as I expected, when beginning to write it.

ADDRESS AND BEHAVIOUR TO YOUR EMPLOYERS

I am now going to give my young friends some advice concerning their behaviour to their employers, &c. In the first place all domestics should be submissive and polite to their employers, and to all visitants that may come to the house. They should never be pert, or strive to enter into conversation with their employers or any visitant that may come to the house, unless they speak to you or ask you a question, and then you should answer them in a polite manner, and in as few words as possible; for you must know that it is a very impertinent thing to strive to force a conversation on your superiors, unless they begin to converse with you first, and then you are to give answers to their questions, if you are versed in the knowledge of whatever may be the subject, and in as correct and polite a manner as possible.

When a lady or gentleman speaks to you, or asks you a question, answer them very kindly, Yes, Ma'am,—or No, Ma'am; Yes, Sir,—or No, Sir. I have often heard servants answer their employ-

ers in such an impertinent manner as to make my blood run
cold, to think that any one should be so ignorant as not to know
his place better; because it is the duty of every servant to be submissive and obedient to their employers; for as the old saying is,
"kind and polite words break no bones"; therefore you should
make it your whole study to be kind and obliging to all around
you, then you are sure to gain credit and esteem from every one.
You should likewise be civil and polite to all visitants who come
to the house, and treat them with as much respect as you would
your own employers, for it is a great advantage to a servant, to
have the good wishes of those ladies and gentlemen that visit
where they live, because you may perhaps one day or other,
have access to their good word, &c.

BEHAVIOUR TO YOUR FELLOW SERVANTS

The greatest comfort of servants is their behaviour and conduct towards each other. You will always find that the more you
endeavour to promote the happiness of those around you, the
more you will secure your own. Never be hasty in passing judg-
ment on any of your comrade servants, as we are all commanded
by our great Creator to act with christian charity towards each
other; and to do unto others as we would they should do unto us,
were we in their situations, and they in ours. If this was the way,
my friends, how much more pleasant our lives would pass away
than they do. But how different the practice is, I have no need to
mention, for time and experience will soon teach us what domestic quarrels are; and I am sorry to say that several families in this
city have such scenes daily to witness. It is there you will see
envy, malice, duplicity, dishonesty, and misrepresentation, and
every evil, to the tormenting of each other, &c. Instead of living
together in unity and affection, and making their home a little
heaven, which they might, if they were so inclined, they make it
a hell on earth, by their wickedness and disagreeable temper, and
often wishing to tyrannize over each other.

I have known several places in Europe, where the servants had
every necessary good to make them comfortable, but yet they
were miserable, all through not agreeing one with the other, as

they should do; wherein is their true happiness, and without which they must live miserable. How much better for servants to live together in peace and happiness, than to be continually quarrelling among themselves; whereas, if they would only yield to each other, and be obliging among one another, they might live as comfortable and more free from care than their employers; as they have many difficulties to encounter from which the servant is free, and sure of his wages. However, it is the lot of all Adam's race to be born to afflictions; servants, therefore, have them more or less, as well as others. At such times we should exercise our charity, and be the more ready to assist each other in cases of sickness or misfortune; as we know not what or how soon it may be our own case. I have known some instances of the good intentions of a kind master towards an afflicted servant often to be frustrated, through the ill nature of the rest of the servants, who would not do any thing for him; thus, the poor afflicted creature is turned out of the house, through the cruelty of his own companions. Such persons as these would do well to consider the words of our Lord and Saviour, as recorded in Matthew, 7th chapter, and 2d verse; "With what measure you mete to others, it shall be measured out to you again." Therefore consider, my young friends, how distressing must be the feelings of a servant when sick, and not able to do his duty any longer; and especially should he be in a foreign country, or far from parents or relations; for relations, we generally have many, but very few friends; and especially at such a period as that, when on a bed of sickness and in poverty.

Now, my young friends, I shall give a few words more of advice. In the first place, my advice is, never to irritate any person that you find to have a contentious spirit, nor hold any argument with such an one. Wherever you may live, strive to live in peace with all; make as many friends as you can, and as few enemies as possible. Watch over your own temper scrupulously; strive not to provoke any person, not even a foolish or conceited person, for if you reprove such, they will certainly hate you, when a wise person would love and respect you. Always watch over the failings of others, as warning to yourself; and always try to do unto others, as you would they should do unto you. Keep this in mind, and it will support you under all your vexations.

Take care and never do an injury to any servant's character, for how easy they may be thrown out of bread through it, and perhaps led to greater evils. Always guard against being influenced to do any kind of injustice to your comrade servants, either by lying, or any other revengeful spirit. Remember that the Lord abhors the deceitful man, and will not let him go unpunished; for Solomon says, "he that uttereth a slander is a fool." And when we recollect that a servant depends wholly on his character for his living, we should be very careful what we say of each other. You should never oppress any, let them be ever so wicked, for good David saith, "God shall break in pieces the oppressor," Psalm 72; and in the 12th, he saith, "For the oppression of the poor and the sighing of the needy, now will I arise, saith the Lord; I will set him in safety, saith the Lord, from him that puffeth at him."

How much better would it be for us to act and do as holy Job did, both for our own comfort and for the comfort of those around us: hear what the good man says in chapter 39th. "I was eyes to the blind, and feet was I to the lame, I was a father to the poor, and the cause which I knew not, I searched out; and I break the jaws of the wicked, and plucked the spoil out of his teeth"; therefore I candidly say unto each of ye, go and do ye likewise, as far as it is in your power so to do, and the Almighty will bring you safe through this wicked world, and place on you a crown of glory in the next: and I sincerely hope that my young friends may study those few hasty remarks and observations which I have here laid down, and now conclude with giving my friends some observations on the behaviour of servants at their meals.

BEHAVIOUR OF SERVANTS
AT THEIR MEALS

Now, my friends, having had the pleasure and gratification of bringing ye in perfect order to wait on your superiors, I will therefore give you some advice and observations on behaviour and propriety at your own meals. In all families there is or should be, a proper time for the meals in the kitchen, so as not to interfere with the parlour hours, as the servants are generally busy at that time. All the help should be ready, if possible, to sit down together at their meals, unless they are hindered by their employers; therefore you should strive to regulate your work, so as to be ready to sit down together, and not be loitering round as some do, which often is the cause of sad contention and confusion; for where one comes now and another at another time, it interferes with the cook's business, and hinders her from her getting her work done in proper season.

Therefore, you should all sit down together thankfully; not to quarrel and dispute with each other, as very often is the case in families, and murmuring that the provisions are not good enough; this I have often seen myself to be the case, with those that had scarcely ever seen or known the comfort of eating a good meal, before they entered a gentleman's service. How wicked must be such conduct towards God, who has made their cups to run over with good things; and how ungrateful must it be to their employers, who provide bountifully to make them comfortable.

In the next place you should always be careful of every thing belonging to your employers, and never make waste of any thing you possibly can avoid. Whenever you draw beer, cider, or the like, for dinner, never draw more than you think is wanted; for it is better to go twice than to make waste, and the old saying is a true one, "that a wilful waste often makes a woful want"; this I have often seen fulfilled, in those that have been extravagant and wasteful of the provisions under their charge.

My young friends, supposing you were in your employer's situation, and servants under your command, and your property in their charge, should you not think them very wicked and dishonest, when wasting your property and provisions? only put this to your own feelings, and it will give you full insight how you should act towards your employers; and how you should manage the property that is put under your trust.

Now, my friends, I shall trespass no longer by these remarks, but give you some few observations how you should conduct yourself at table, when at meals. Make it your study always to be clean at meal times; never talk much while eating; be polite and help all round, before yourself. Never begin any vulgar conversation at such or any time. I have known some servants that were so rude, and void of all discretion, as to use the most vulgar conversation during meal times, which was a disgrace to any being, and ought not to be suffered in a gentleman's family. Always behave respectfully, and never stand up before the others are done, unless your business calls you. When done dinner, put by your chair; never leave your things about for others to wait on you, for in this station every one should attend to their own business. When done, you should always offer up a blessing for the good you have received; for we are ordered by the Lord to receive every thing with thanksgiving and prayer; therefore, my friends, I sincerely hope that these examples will become beneficial to all who may study them. I shall now conclude these remarks and instructions, and give some hints to servants in general on their dress.

HINTS TO HOUSE SERVANTS
ON THEIR DRESS

Now, David, in the first place I shall address myself particularly to you, and give you a few hasty remarks on the propriety of servants in dressing, &c. There is no class of people that should dress more neat and clean than a house servant, because he is generally exposed to the eyes of the public; but his dress, though neat and tidy, should not be foppish, or extravagant. A man that lives in a family should have two or three changes of light clothes for the summer, that he may always appear neat and clean. You should likewise have a good suit of clothes on purpose to wear while waiting on dinner, as there is nothing that looks more creditable than to see a servant well dressed at dinner. It is a credit to himself and the family whom he has the honor to serve. Make it a rule always to brush your dinner suit, when your morning's work is done, and every thing put in order, that you may have them ready when you want to dress for dinner.

You should never wear thick shoes or boots in the parlour, or waiting on dinner. You should have a pair of light pumps, on purpose for dinner, and a pair of slippers is the best thing you can wear in the morning, as they are easy to your feet while running about and doing your morning's work; likewise you are free from making a noise to disturb the family before they are up. You must always be very clean in your person, and wash your face and comb your hair, &c.

In the next place wash your feet at least three times per week, as in summer time your feet generally perspire; a little weak vinegar and water, or a little rum is very good for this use, as it is a stimulant, and there is no danger of taking cold after washing in either. Servants being generally on the foot throughout the day, it must cause perspiration, which makes a bad smell, which would be a very disagreeable thing to yourself and the company on whom you wait.

Now, David, there is one thing more that I must caution you against, that is, running in debt for fine clothes, &c. There are many servants that practise this to their utter ruin, all through pride and vanity, striving even to outvie their master. This is a very unbecoming thing in a servant, and no one would do so but an ignorant person and one that does not know his place; because, in the first place, his circumstances do not allow it. I never find fault with a servant to dress well, and always to be clean and tidy, but he should not be extravagant, or go above his ability. I have known several servants who dressed so foppish that it looked quite ridiculous, and myself have seen those very same servants afterwards in a perfect state of poverty, and without a dollar to help themselves. Consider, my young friend, that when sickness comes on, and no friends or relations to look to you, and no money laid up to support you, then what good does all your fine clothes? does not your pride then make you repent of your folly, and wish that you had been more careful of your money; instead of spending it to support your ignorant pride and folly? It absolutely makes me think of the fable of the frog and the ox; where the poor conceited frog puffed himself up, thinking to be as large as the ox, but at length he burst. This was all through pride and folly; and this I compare to a servant that strives to be in fashion, and spends all his money; then sickness comes on, and he sinks in poverty and death, and is no more thought of after, than the poor frog. But, my young friend, I sincerely hope that this never may be the case with you, or any other that has to earn a living in this capacity; for the holy scripture says, that "the servant must not be above his master"; therefore I hope you will follow those examples.

––––––––

REMARKS ON ANSWERING THE BELLS

This is a part of a house servant's business, that requires a great deal of attention. Whenever your parlour or drawing room bell rings, lose no time in going to answer it; never wait to finish what you are about, and leave the bell unanswered; you never should let the bell ring twice if you possibly can avoid it, for it seems to be a great part of negligence in a servant, besides, it is an aggravating thing to those who ring twice or thrice without being answered. In the next place, when your front door bell rings, you must always step quick to answer it, before it ring the second time; because perhaps it might be some person of distinction, or on some business of great importance to your employers, wherein no one coming to answer the bell, they might go away and think that the family are not at home.

In the next place, you should never admit any person or persons into the parlour or drawing room, without first announcing their names to your mistress or master. This you can readily find out by saying, "What name shall I say, ma'am?" or "sir?" Therefore by this way you will find out whether your employers wish to see them or not. If not, tell them your mistress, master, or whoever they wish to see, are engaged, &c. in a polite and civil manner.

Now, my friend, I have brought you so far as to be able to understand the whole duty of a house servant perfectly. I shall give you in the following pages, all the useful receipts that are requisite for a house servant to understand, and to enable him to do every part of his work with expedition and to perfection.

All those receipts that I am going to lay before you and the public, are of my own long experience, which I can recommend to be genuine, as to every thing they are set to; and you will find them to be genuine.

RECEIPTS

1.—TO MAKE THE BEST LIQUID BLACKING

Take two quarts of sour beer or porter, the latter is preferable, eight ounces of best ivory black, three ounces of molasses, one ounce of sugar candy, half an ounce of gum arabic, half an ounce of oil of vitriol, and one ounce of sweet oil. Let your ivory black be well rubbed, to become fine and free from lumps; mix the oil with the black, and dissolve the gum-arabic in some warm beer, then mix all the ingredients well together, keep it corked tight, in a jar or what you choose to put it in, shake it well three or four times each day for two or three days, then it will be fit for use; and if used as the directions are given in boot and shoe cleaning, it will produce a brilliant and jet black, and is not in the least any way injurious to leather.

2.—TO MAKE BOOTS OR SHOES WATER PROOF

Take one pint of drying oil, two ounces of good yellow wax, two ounces of turpentine, (not spirits of turpentine,) half an ounce of burgundy pitch, melt all these ingredients carefully over some hot coals, be careful that the blaze does not get to it, or it will catch afire; when they are all melted well together, take a painter's brush, or a piece of flannel tied on the end of a stick, then apply your stuff on the boots or shoes as hot as possible without burning them, set them some distance from the fire, and when they become dry, apply the stuff on again as before, and so on until the leather will become saturated and hold no more; then put them by for some time before you use them, until they become dry and elastic; this method will make them impenetrable to wet or snow, and make them soft and of much more durability.

3.—TO CLEAN MAHOGANY FURNITURE

Take one pound, or whatever quantity you choose, of best yellow wax, scrape it very fine, then put it into a pot or pipkin for that purpose, pour over it as much spirits of turpentine as will cover it well, you must let it stand 24 hours before you use it. If your furniture is to be perfectly clear and light coloured, you may not add any thing to it. But if it is required to be of a dark colour, you may add to it half an ounce of rose pink, or alkanet root in fine powder, mix them well together, and with a soft brush, or piece of flannel, rub quite even over the tables, or whatever furniture you are going to clean, rub quick and even, and polish off with a piece of flannel, and an old silk handkerchief afterwards.

4.—FURNITURE OIL FOR MAHOGANY

Take one pint of cold strained linseed oil, half an ounce of alkanet root, half an ounce of rose pink, put them into a bottle or jar, shake it up well together. It will be fit for use in twenty-four hours; you must be very careful when putting it on your furniture; apply it on with a piece of woollen cloth or flannel, and put it very even over your furniture, rub it very quick and hard, until it is perfectly worked in, then polish off with linen cloths, and you will soon have a beautiful polish; you must be careful and rub the edges of your tables very clean, that the ladies or gentlemen may not get their clothes soiled.

5.—ITALIAN VARNISH, MOST SUPERB FOR FURNITURE

Melt one part of virgin wax (white) in eight parts of oil petroleum, lay a light coat of this very even over your furniture while warm, you may put it on with a badger's brush; let it stand for ten or fifteen minutes, then polish off with a piece of coarse soft cloth or flannel, and finish with an old silk handkerchief. Inexperienced servants should be very careful how they apply any receipt at first, they should always make the first experiment on some article of little value.

6.—ITALIAN POLISH FOR GIVING FURNITURE A BRILLIANT LUSTRE

First, melt one quarter of a pound of best yellow wax, and one ounce of black rosin well pounded to powder, put them into a pipkin, or something else for that purpose, then pour over them, by degrees, two ounces spirits of turpentine; then mix it well together and cover it close for use. You may apply this on your furniture with a piece of soft woollen cloth, or some new flannel, be careful and put it on even and light, finish off with a piece of old silk or a handkerchief; in a few applications this will produce a most brilliant and hard polish, and is not so liable to be stained by the heat of the dishes, as any other polish now in use, but looks as beautiful as the finest varnish.

7.—TO TAKE INK STAINS OUT OF MAHOGANY

Dilute one teaspoonful of oil of vitriol in one tablespoonful of soft water, apply it to the parts affected, with a small piece of red flannel, rub rather light and quick until the spot disappears, then wash off with a little milk; rub quick until dry, then apply your polish, &c. Spirits of salts will answer the same purpose.

8.—AN EXCELLENT ARTICLE FOR TABLES, AFTER PARTIES, &c.

Take one pint of milk, one ounce of spirits of turpentine, two dessert spoonsful of sweet oil, mix them well together, put the mixture into a bottle for use. When your tables are very dirty and stained with wine and fruit, after a party, &c. shake up your mixture and pour some out into an old saucer, or any thing you may have for that purpose, Dip into a piece of flannel, and wash your tables quick and even all over, then dry and polish off with some old linen cloths. By this method, your tables will become a fine light colour, and will look most beautiful when cleaned off with your furniture oil, polish, or varnish.

9.—TO TAKE THE BLACK OFF THE BARS OF POLISHED STEEL GRATES

Take one pound of soft soap, one quart of rain or soft water, put them in a sauce pan and boil it down to one pint, then take some of this jelly and mix it with some emery No. 3, and apply it to the bars of your grate with a piece of coarse cloth. Rub hard and quick, and it will remove the black in a few minutes.

10.—TO POLISH THE BRIGHT BARS OF POLISHED STEEL GRATES, OR FIRE IRONS

Take some rotten-stone finely powdered, mix with it some spirits of turpentine, one teaspoonful of oil of vitriol, one table-spoonful of sweet oil; mix all well together, and apply it with a piece of coarse woollen cloth to the bars of your grate; rub hard and quick, wipe off with old linen or cotton cloths, and polish with some dry rotten-stone and a piece of leather.

11.—THE BEST WAY TO CLEAN A POLISHED STEEL GRATE

After you have removed the black from off the bars, take one ounce of crocus, one tablespoonful of sweet oil, mix well together, then add spirits of wine or Hollands gin, by degrees, until your mixture is to the consistency of paint, then apply it to your grate or fire irons, hard and quick, with a piece of coarse woollen cloth; wipe off with old linen or cotton cloth, and polish with dry whiting and leather. This receipt, if properly applied, gives a most brilliant polish, and repairs brightness of steel, and stands the fire much better than any now in use.

12.—FOR THE BLACK PARTS OR INNER HEARTH OF A GRATE

Take some best black lead finely powdered, add to it the whites of three eggs well beaten, then pour into it some sour beer, or porter, the latter is preferable, mix it well together, to the consistency of liquid blacking, then these ingredients must be simmered over some hot coals for twenty minutes; when cold, pour it into a junk bottle for use; apply it on your grate with a soft brush, and polish off quick in the same manner as you would a boot. This will give a beautiful polish, and hold for some time, by dusting it off in the morning, after you make your fire, with an old cloth, and then with your hard brush.

13.—ANOTHER EXCELLENT BLACK MIXTURE FOR THE SAME

Take some good black lead finely powdered, mix with three sour apples beat up to a paste, then pour on some good vinegar till it is to the consistency of blacking, and apply it in the same manner as the preceding receipt; this will give a beautiful polish.

14.—A BEAUTIFUL SECRET TO CLEAN BRASS OR COPPER

Dissolve in one quart of rain or soft water, one ounce of oxalic acid, shake it well up together, then add half an ounce of butter of antimony; bottle it and cork close for use. This composition will not soil any thing it touches, it is excellent for cleaning the brass on bureaus, or the brass of the front door, &c. It will likewise take stains out of mahogany; this must be applied with a piece of mantle cloth, or white flannel is preferable as it is soft;

wipe off quick with a soft linen cloth, and polish with leather. This will stand the heat of the fire better than any method in use, and is clean for the hands, or any thing it touches. Always shake it up before use.

––––––

15.—TO GIVE BRITANNIA METAL A BEAUTIFUL POLISH

Take half a pound of lump whiting, as it is free from grit or sand, scrape it and roll it into fine powder, then add to it one wine glass full of sweet oil, and one tablespoonful of soft soap; mix these well together, then add, by degrees, some New-England rum, or spirits of wine, to the consistency of cream. Apply it to the article with a soft sponge or piece of flannel, quick and even; wipe off with a piece of old linen or cotton cloth, dust over some dry whiting and polish with leather.

––––––

16.—ANOTHER BEAUTIFUL POLISH FOR BLACK GRATES

Take the whites of six eggs, beat them up to a froth, then add half a pound of black lead, mix well together, then add spirits of turpentine until it is to the consistency of liquid blacking; apply it with a brush as you would black a boot. Polish with a hard brush, and it will become a brilliant polish.

––––––

17.—TO MAKE THE BEST PLATE POWDER

Take half a pound of chalk, scrape it and roll it into powder, then sift it through a fine sieve, then mix into it half an ounce of quicksilver; when well mixed, add two ounces of hartshorn balls in fine powder, then mix all extremely well together. To use this, take some of this powder and apply it to your plate with your naked hand, observing to rub it well and even all over; then polish off with your leather; or take some of the powder and work it into your shammy leather, and rub your plate perfectly well and even, and polish as the other. The best way to use this is to make it wet, as you can apply it more even, and is much the safest way for new beginners; to wet this properly, take some spirits of wine and wet it until it becomes to the consistency of cream, then take a piece of soft sponge, and rub your plate well and even all over. Wipe off with your leather and polish with a clean leather; this will give your plate a most beautiful lustre. Once a week is enough to clean with this powder, hot soap suds may be used at other times.

18.—ANOTHER WAY, MOST SUPERB, TO CLEAN PLATE

Dissolve in one quart of rain or soft water, one ounce of prepared hartshorn powder, mix it well together, and put it into a saucepan on some hot coals, so as to be scalding hot, then put into it as much plate as the vessel may hold, that they may be covered, let it boil a little, then take it out and drain it over the saucepan, and let it dry before the fire, then put in some more, and so on until you have it all done; then put in some clean linen rags and leave them to soak up all the water; these will be excellent to clean the plates of doors or any kind of brasses. Polish your silver when dry, with soft leather.

19.—ANOTHER EXCELLENT PLATE POWDER, BY J. R. W. LONDON

Take one ounce of zinc, melt it in an iron ladle, then put to it two ounces of quicksilver, then turn this mixture out on some strong brown paper, pound and roll it fine, then pound and sift two pounds of best cake whiting, mix them well together, then mix in half an ounce of good vermilion, rub and mix them well up together. If you choose to use it wet, add to some of the powder spirits of wine, sufficient to make it the thickness of cream; rub your plate well and even with a piece of soft sponge dipped in this mixture, and polish off with your shammy leather. This powder, if properly made and used, will give a most brilliant and elegant lustre to silver, &c.

20.—TO CLEAN PLATED ARTICLES
OF ALL DESCRIPTIONS

Take one ounce of killed quicksilver, this you may get at the apothecaries, mix with this half a pound of best cake whiting pounded and sifted, then dried before you put in the quicksilver. When dry, mix these well together, and put the powder into a bottle for use; when your plated things want cleaning, take a little of this powder and wet it with some spirits of wine, or New-England gin, and rub the articles lightly over with a soft sponge. Once a fortnight is sufficient for plated ware to be cleaned with this powder. Good hot and strong soap suds is the best to use for plated ware, the rest of the time, and to be wiped quick out of the hot suds, with soft cloths, and polished after with your shammy leather.

21.—TO CLEAN JAPANNED
TEA AND COFFEE URNS

Take one ounce of crocus, and half an ounce of rotten-stone, pound and mix them well together, then sift it, let this mixture be a little darker than the urns. You need not use rotten-stone if you can get the crocus powder dark enough. Clean your urns with this powder, as directed for cleaning plate, &c.

22.—TO PRESERVE IRON OR
STEEL FROM RUSTING

Take a piece of mutton suet, the skin part that is over the kidneys is the best for this purpose; rub the bars of your grate or fire irons well over with this, then take some fresh unslacked lime, put it into a piece of muslin and dust it well over whatever you have to preserve. By this method you may preserve iron or steel for many months, and no damp can penetrate to them. Fire arms should be kept well wrapped up in baize, or paper, and laid by in a dry place. This is an excellent way to preserve best knives that you wish to lay by for any length of time, or that are to be exported.

23.—TO TAKE RUST OUT OF STEEL, &c.

Rub your steel that is rusty well over with a piece of flannel dipped in salad oil, no other oil will answer, as there generally is water in all other kinds. When you have rubbed them well over with the oil, then shake a little hot slacked lime over them and let them lay in a dry place for 48 hours; then take some fresh unslacked lime finely powdered, and rub quick and hard until the rust disappears; then polish off with dry whiting, or crocus, and shammy leather. This is a most excellent plan, if only properly done, as is here directed.

24.—TO BLACKEN THE FRONT OF STONE CHIMNEY PIECES

Mix oil, varnish, spirits of turpentine, and lampblack, thin it to the consistency of thin paint, wash the stone very clean with hot soap suds, sponge it off with clean warm water, then when perfectly dry, take a painter's brush and put on a very smooth coat, let that dry, then put on another, observe to sift the lampblack before used, and this will give a most beautiful appearance, and look like varnish.

25.—ANOTHER EXCELLENT WAY TO CLEAN BLACK GRATES

Boil one quarter of a pound of best black lead in one pint of beer or porter, add one tablespoonful of good soft soap; when it boils, take it off the fire, and when you are going to polish your grate, brush off all the dust from it, and with a painter's brush apply this mixture quite even on the grate, then polish it off quick with a hard brush, and you will have a beautiful appearance to your grate.

26.—TO CLEAN MIRRORS
AND LOOKING GLASSES

Clean off the fly stains and other soils, with a piece of soft flannel dipped in gin, wipe dry with soft linen cloths, and polish off with a soft dry flannel and powder blue; finish with a silk handkerchief; this is an excellent way to clean all kinds of looking glasses, &c.

The author had this receipt from one of the largest looking glass manufacturers in London.

27.—TO MAKE A BEAUTIFUL BLACK VARNISH

Take gum lac four ounces, sanderach and black rosin, of each one ounce, pulverize all separately; dissolve the rosin in a sufficient quantity of spirits of wine, then add the sanderach; as soon as dissolved add the powder of gum lac; mix them all well together, and strain the mixture through a thin linen cloth. The black colour is to be given by mixing into it drachms of ivory black.

28.—TO GIVE SILVER A BEAUTIFUL POLISH

Scrape very fine four ounces of good white soap, pour on it one pint of rain or soft water, scalding not, dissolve in that water half an ounce of wine ley dried in cakes, (this you will get at the apothecaries) and the same quantity of pearl ashes; mix them all well together, apply it with a sponge on your silver, and wash off in hot soap suds, and dry off with hot cloths, which you must have hung before the fire for that purpose; afterwards polish with your shammy leather.

29.—AN EXCELLENT MASTICK FOR
MENDING GLASS, CHINA, &c.

Take whites of eggs, soft curd cheese, and quicklime, of each an equal quantity in weight, then begin and beat them all well together until the mastick becomes quite smooth; this may be used in most all kinds of ware; it will cement broken glass, so as to stand fire or hot water without having the smallest effect on the part cemented, but stand like new.

30.—A WASH TO REVIVE OLD DEEDS, OR OTHER WRITINGS

Boil gall nuts in white wine, and steep a sponge in this solution, then pass it smoothly over the old writings, &c. and they will appear directly as new as when first wrote.

31.—AN EXCELLENT WAY TO PREVENT FLIES FROM SETTLING ON PICTURES, OR MAKING DIRT ON FURNITURE

Take a large bunch of leeks and soak them in a pail of soft water for 24 hours, then squeeze the leeks out of the water, let it stand for half an hour, then strain it off and bottle for use; in the fly season take a sponge and wash your pictures or any furniture whatever, with this solution, and the flies will never come near it, or make any dirt on it. This is a valuable receipt for private families, &c.

32.—TO REMOVE FLIES FROM ROOMS

Take half a teaspoonful of black pepper, in powder, one teaspoonful of brown sugar, and one tablespoonful of cream; mix them well together, and place them in the room, on a plate, where the flies are troublesome, and they will soon disappear.

33.—TO RENDER OLD PICTURES AS FINE AS NEW

Boil in a new pipkin for the space of one quarter of an hour, one quarter of a pound of bril, or grey ash, and a little Genoa soap; when it is lukewarm take a soft piece of sponge and pass it even all over your pictures; when dry, pass over it very lightly some olive die, and in five minutes wipe it off with a piece of old silk, or soft linen cloth; this will make your pictures look as well, and have as fine a gloss, as when new.

34.—A VARNISH WHICH SUITS ALL KINDS OF PICTURES AND PRINTS, AND MAKES THEM SHINE LIKE GLASS

Dilute one quarter of a pound of Venice turpentine in one gill of spirits of wine, if too thick, add some more spirits of wine, until of the consistency of milk, then lay one coat of this on the right side of the print or picture, and when dry it will shine like glass; if not to your satisfaction, lay on another coat, and it will have a most brilliant effect.

35.—TO TAKE INK SPOTS OUT OF MAHOGANY

Take a piece of clean white flannel, dip it into some spirits of salts, apply it quick to the part affected, until removed, then wash it off with a little cream or milk, and rub off dry; don't let it stand too long on it.

36.—A MOST DELICIOUS SALAD SAUCE, BY J. R. W.

Take the yolks of four hard-boiled eggs, rub them through a sieve, and add to them one teaspoonful of salt, mix well up, then add two tablespoonsful of made mustard, stir well up, then add by one spoonful at each time, six spoonsful of salad oil; mix this well together until it becomes as smooth as mustard, then put in one teaspoonful of anchovy sauce, and one gill of cream or new milk, and stir well together; and last of all put in by degrees some good vinegar; I don't state the quantity of this, as some is much stronger than others, this must lay in your own taste. Should you make it too sharp with vinegar, add one tablespoonful of fine white sugar in powder, this will soften it, and give it an excellent flavour. Bottle it for use. This will keep for any length of time, in the hottest weather; and is excellent with any kind of salad or boiled slaw, and is a fine relish with fish. Shake it well up before you put it on your salad.

37.—A GREAT SECRET TO MIX MUSTARD, BY M. B. OF LONDON

Take one quart of water that corned beef has been boiled in, skim off any fat that may remain, then strain it and when cool put it into a junk bottle, then grate some horseradish, about two dessert spoonsful, and put into the bottle and shake it well up, and cork it tight. When you want to mix your mustard, take whatever quantum you think necessary, but you should never mix more than half your mustard pot full at once, as it is better when first mixed; first put the flour of mustard in a tea-cup, add to it half a teaspoonful of salt, mix well together, then put in your liquor, by degrees, that you may not make it too thin, mix extremely well together, until it becomes quite smooth; this method of mixing mustard is absolutely the best I have ever met with, as it much surpasses any other, both in strength and flavour.

38.—TO EXTRACT OIL FROM BOARDS

Make a strong ley of pearl ashes and soft water, then add some fresh unslacked lime, stir it extremely well together, then let it stand for fifteen minutes, and bottle it off, and cork it close. Before you use it, have some water ready to lower it, as it generally is very powerful; then scour the part affected and rinse it with clean soft water. Don't let the liquor lay too long on the part affected, or it will remove the colour from the board, &c. therefore you must do it with care and expedition.

39.—TO COLOUR ANY KIND OF LIQUOR

Take, in coarse powder, half an ounce of santulum rubium, put it into a bottle of a quart measure, then pour on the powder three half pints of spirits of wine, and in five or six hours it will be a very high tincture, and will be fit to give a colour to any kind of liquid that you choose, by pouring some of it into the liquor and shaking it very well.

40.—TO MAKE A LIQUID CURRANT JAM, OF THE FIRST QUALITY

Take four pounds of clean picked currants, put aside two and a half pounds of them, and squeeze the remainder; then put this in a preserving pan, with four pounds of sugar; when come to a syrup, put in the remainder of the whole currants along with the one and a half pounds of juice, and boil it to the greatest perfection.

41.—A SECRET AGAINST ALL KINDS OF SPOTS ON CLOTH OR SILK, OF ANY COLOUR

Take a water impregnated with alkaline salt, black soap, and bullock's gall; this composition will take out any kind of spots from any kind of cloth, silk, &c. Rinse off with soft warm water.

42.—HOW TO MAKE ALL KINDS OF SYRUPS, WITH ALL SORTS OF FLOWERS

Heat in a pan half a pint of water, then put into it sugar to the quantity of flowers; boil, skim, and thicken it to a proper consistency; when done, put it into a glazed pot or pan and cover it over with a linen cloth, through which pour the syrup upon the flowers; these being deadened, put altogether again into the same piece of linen, and squeeze them; strain it into another vessel, then bottle and cork it close; the quantity of sugar requisite for this syrup is generally one pound and a half to every four ounces of flowers. Observe that all kinds of flowers must be picked and cleaned of their cups and stems, and nothing but their leaves made use of.

43.—TO MAKE AN EXCELLENT CURRANT JELLY

Dissolve in water four pounds of loaf sugar to a strong syrup, then take four pounds of clean picked currants, then put them into the syrup, and boil so as to have them covered with the bubbles; after six minutes such a boil, take the pan from the fire, and pour the contents into a sieve, strain off all the liquor, then put this liquor again into the pan, and when you want to try it, take a little with the skimmer and put it on a plate, if it congeals as it cools, it is fit to pot.

N. B. Those who want to spare sugar and have a great quantity of syrup or jelly, at a small expense, may apply only four pounds of sugar to six pounds of currants, only observing to do it rather more than in the manner above; and by this method you will save a great deal of expense in making a large quantity of jelly.

44.—A MOST DELICIOUS LEMONADE, TO BE MADE THE DAY BEFORE WANTED

Take and pare two dozen of good sized lemons as thin as you possibly can; put eight of the rinds into three quarts of hot water, but not boiling, cover it close over four hours, then rub some sugar to the rinds to attract the essence, and put it into a bowl, and into which squeeze the juice of the lemons; to which add one pound and a half of fine sugar, then put the water to the above, and three quarts of boiling milk, mix and run through a jelly bag until clear; bottle it, if you choose, and cork close; this will be most excellent, and will keep.

45.—LEMONADE THAT HAS THE
APPEARANCE AND FLAVOUR OF JELLY

Pare two Seville oranges, and six lemons, as thin as possible, steep them for four hours in one quart of hot water, then boil one pound and a quarter of loaf sugar in three pints of water, skim it, and then add the two liquors to the juice of six good oranges, and twelve lemons: stir the whole well together, and run it through a jelly bag until clear, then add a little orange water, if you like the flavour, and if wanted, you may add more sugar; if corked tight it will keep a long time.

46.—TO MAKE RASPBERRY
VINEGAR MOST DELICIOUS

Put one quart of clean picked raspberries into a large bowl, pour on them one quart of best white wine vinegar, the next day strain off the liquor on one pound of fresh raspberries, and the following day do the same, but do not squeeze the fruit, but drain the liquor as dry as possible from the fruit; the last time pass it through a cloth wet in vinegar, to prevent any waste, then put it into a stone jar, with a pound of sugar to every pint of juice, let your sugar be in large lumps, as it is much better; when dissolved stir it up well, put your jar in a pot of hot water, let it simmer, skim well, and when cold bottle and cork close.

47.—TO MAKE BEST WINE
VINEGAR IN ONE HOUR

Take some rye flour and dilute it with some of the best and strongest vinegar you can find, make a thin round cake, bake it in the oven, then pound it into fine powder, then wet it as before, and bake again; repeat this operation three or four times, then if you hang the last made cake while hot, by a cord, in a cask of wine, you will have most excellent vinegar in one hour.

48.—AN EXCELLENT PREPARATION FOR VINEGAR

Take white cinnamon, long pepper, and cyprus, of each one ounce, round pepper half an ounce, and two nutmegs; pulverize each article separate, and put them into so many different bags, then take five quarts of the best vinegar, put into each quart one of the bags, and boil separately each quart for three minutes, and so on until all are done, observing to keep each quart and bag by itself in different vessels; then boil separately six quarts of best wine, then season your cask by rinsing it out with vinegar, then pour in your boiled wines and vinegars, and then half fill your cask with the worst spoiled wine, and stop it up until the vinegar is made, then draw off what you please, but fill up again with the same quantity that you draw off, of your bad wine; by this process you can draw off and fill again for a number of times, and it will be a most excellent flavoured vinegar.

49.– A DRY PORTABLE VINEGAR, OR VINAIGRE EN POUDRE

Wash clean in warm water one pound of white tartar, dry it and powder it as fine as possible, wet this with the best sharp vinegar, dry it in an oven after the bread comes out, or before the fire, powder and wet it as before, and so on for ten or a dozen times, and you will have an excellent vinegar powder that will turn water into vinegar; this is excellent for travelling parties to carry with them.

50.—TO TURN GOOD WINE INTO VINEGAR IN THREE HOURS

Put into any quantity of wine you choose, say one gallon for the experiment, one red beet, and in three hours, it will be sour and true vinegar. By J. R. W.

51.—TO RESTORE THAT SAME WINE
TO ITS FIRST TASTE

Take out the beet, and in its stead put a clean cabbage root, and it will return to its primary taste in the same space of time.

52.—TO CORRECT A BAD TASTE OR
SOURNESS IN WINE

Put into a clean linen bag one or two roots of wild horseradish cut in fine pieces, let it hang down through the bung hole into the wine, by a piece of twine, let it stay there for two days, then take that out, and put in another in the same manner, and repeat until the wine is perfectly restored.

53.—TO PRESERVE GOOD WINE TO THE LAST

Take the bulk of your two fists of the inside bark of the alder tree, which is green, pour on it one pint of the best spirits of wine, let this infuse for three days, then strain it off through a linen cloth, then pour this infusion into a hogshead of wine, this wine will keep for twelve years, or longer, if wanted.

54.—TO RECOVER A PERSON
FROM INTOXICATION

Make the person that is intoxicated drink a glass of vinegar, or a cup of strong coffee without milk or sugar, or a glass of hot wine. Any of those articles are a most safe and quick remedy to recover a person from intoxication.

55.—TO MAKE RASPBERRY, STRAWBERRY, CHERRY, AND ALL KINDS OF WATERS

Take any quantity of the ripest raspberries, squeeze them through a linen cloth, to extract the juice from them, put this in a glass bottle uncorked placed in the sun or on a stove until it is cleared down, then pour it gently into another bottle without disturbing the sediment, to half a pint of this put one quart of water, and sugar to your taste, pour it from one vessel to the other, strain it, and put it in ice to cool, this will be a most delicious cool drink in hot weather, and extremely safe in perspirations.

56.—LEMONADE WATER OF A DELICIOUS FLAVOUR

Dissolve one pound of loaf sugar in two quarts of water, grate over it the yellow of five large lemons, then mix in twelve drops of essential oil of sulphur, when going to mix your liquid, cut thin some slices of lemons, and keep it cool and it will be most excellent.

57.—ANOTHER EXCELLENT LEMONADE, BY R. R., THE AUTHOR OF THIS BOOK

Take one gallon of water, put to it the juice of ten good lemons, and the zeasts of six of them likewise, then add to this one pound of sugar, and mix it well together, strain it through a fine strainer, and put it in ice to cool; this will be a most delicious and fine lemonade.

58.—TO WHITEN IVORY
THAT HAS BEEN SPOILED

Take some soft water, dissolve in it a sufficient quantity of rock alum, so as to render the water quite milky, then boil this liquor, then soak the handles of your knives, forks, &c. for one hour, then take an old tooth brush and brush them well over, after which wrap them in a wet linen cloth to dry leisurely, otherwise it is apt to split. This is an excellent plan to whiten ivory.

59.—A COOLING CINNAMON WATER
IN HOT WEATHER

Boil one gallon of water, pour it into a gallon demijohn, set this before the fire, then put into it twelve cloves, two ounces of whole cinnamon, then stop up your bottle and put it in a cool place; when you want to mix your liquor, put half a pint into two quarts of water, with one quarter of a pound of sugar; cool it in ice before you serve it, and it is a most wholesome and delicious drink as you can take in hot weather.

60.—AN EXCELLENT GOOD
RATIFIA, BY F. N.

Into one quart of brandy pour half a pint of cherry juice, as much of currant juice, as much of raspberry juice, add a few cloves, and some white pepper in grains, two grains of green coriander, and a stick or two of cinnamon, then pound the stones of the cherries, and put them in, wood and all. Add about twenty five or thirty kernels of apricots. Stop your demijohn close, and let it infuse for one month in the shade, shaking it five or six times in that time, at the end of which strain it through a flannel bag, then through a filtering paper, and then bottle it and cork close for use; you can make any quantity you choose, only by adding or increasing more brandy or other ingredients, &c.

61.—A STRONG ANISE-SEED WATER

Take half a pint of the best essential spirits of anise seeds, put this into three quarts of the best brandy, with one quart of boiled water; if not sweet enough, add some clarified sugar, and strain through a jelly bag, this is a most delicious and wholesome water, and a fine stomachic.

62.—TO TAKE OFF SPOTS OF ANY SORT, FROM ANY KIND OF CLOTH

Take half a pound of crude honey, the yoke of a new laid egg, and the bulk of a nut of aromatic salt, then mix all well together, then put some on the spots; having left it there awhile, then wash it off with clean water, and the spot will immediately disappear. This receipt is of great importance to servants that have the care of their master's wardrobe, and in many other similar cases.

63.—A SECRET AGAINST OIL SPOTS, &C.

Take a piece of white soap, shave it very fine, put it into a junk bottle with rather a wide neck and mouth, half fill it with ley, then add to this the bulk of a nut of ammoniac salt, and two yolks of fresh eggs, cabbage juice and bullock's gall, of each half an ounce weight, and one ounce of salt of tartar in fine powder; cork your bottle close, and lay it in the sun for four days, after which it will be fit for use. You must apply this to the oil spot with a piece of white flannel, rub hard and quick, let it stand five or ten minutes afterwards, then rinse off with clean soft water, and hang out to dry.

64.—TO RESTORE CARPETS
TO THEIR FIRST BLOOM

Beat your carpets with your carpet rods until perfectly clean from dust, then if there be any ink spots take it out with a lemon, and if oil spots, take out as in the foregoing receipt, observing to rinse with clean water; then take a hot loaf of white bread, split down the centre, having the top and bottom crust one on each half, with this rub your carpet extremely well over, then hang it out on or across a line with the right side out; should the night be fine, leave it out all night, and if the weather be clear, leave it out for two or three such nights, then sweep it with a clean corn broom, and it will look as when first new.

65.—TO RESTORE TAPESTRIES TO
THEIR FORMER BRIGHTNESS

Shake and dust your tapestries extremely well, then rub them well and even all over with white chalk, which you must leave on them for twenty-four hours; then take a hair brush and brush off all the chalk, then apply all your chalk as before, and let them stand as before, after which, beat them well with a light rod, and afterwards brush them well and even with a soft clothes-brush, and this operation will make them look as bright and clear as if quite new.

66.—TO REVIVE THE COLOUR OF CLOTH

Pour one quart of soft water on one pound of burnt pot-ashes, in twelve hours after pour it off in another vessel, then put in a handful of marsh mallow leaves, with two bullocks' galls; boil these altogether until the leaves go to the bottom, then set this decoction in the sun for four days, afterwards take whatever colour you want, boil it with the cloth in the liquor, and let it soak in the liquor for twelve days, and the colour of the cloth will be restored, as prime as ever.

67.—TO TAKE SPOTS OUT OF WHITE CLOTHES

Boil in one pint of soft water for half an hour two ounces of alum, then put in two ounces of white soap scraped fine, and one pound of alum, let it boil for five minutes longer, then take it up and let it stand in the cool for four days, then bottle it, and with this composition you can take out any kind of spots whatever from white cloth. Apply this with a piece of white flannel, rubbing the spots hard and quick, afterwards rinse with clean soft water, let the garment or piece of cloth hang out in the air one or two clear days and nights.

68.—A COMPOSITION OF SOAP THAT WILL TAKE OUT ALL KINDS OF SPOTS

Take one pound of Venetian white soap, six yolks of eggs, and one dessert-spoonful of salt in fine powder; incorporate these all well together, then add a sufficient quantity of the juice of the leaves of white beet; then make up this composition into small cakes, which dry in the shade. To apply these, first wet the spot over with clean soft water, then rub it over on both sides with the soap, then let it be rinsed in clean water, and the spots will disappear, hang out to dry, and afterwards brush it.

69.—TURKEY CEMENT FOR JOINING METALS, GLASS, &c.

Dissolve six pieces of mastick as large as common sized peas, in as much spirits of wine as is sufficient to make it into a liquid; in another vessel dissolve as much isinglass which has previously soaked in soft water until soft, in brandy, as will make two ounces in weight of strong glue, then add two small pieces of ammonium which must be rubbed until dissolved, then heat all up together; when cool, put it into a phial and stop it close, when you want to use it put the phial into warm water not boiling, apply it with a thin piece of stick formed as a knife, for that purpose.

70.—TO PRESERVE THE
BRIGHTNESS OF ARMS, &c.

Take some strong vinegar, that of Montpelier is best, dissolve in this some alum finely powdered, then rub the arms with this composition, keep them in a dry place, and they will keep bright for years. This is an excellent thing to preserve the brightness of polished steel grates, or fire irons, &c.

71.—TO REMOVE INK STAINS FROM CLOTH,
PLAID, SILK OR WORSTED, &c.

Take one pint of rain or other soft water, dissolve in it half an ounce of oxalic, citric, or tartaric acid; the half ounce will be sufficient to mix the pint strong enough, cork it very close and shake it well; to use it, lay the part affected over a bowl of hot water, but not to touch the water, and let the steam evaporate through, then shake up the solution and dip a sponge into it, and rub well the part affected until the stain disappears, then hang it out in the sun, and this solution will not hurt the finest fabric.

72.—TO PRESERVE MILK FOR SEA,
TO KEEP SIX MONTHS

Take as many bottles as you wish to fill, wash and dry them very clean, then fill them right from the cows' teats; after you have them all full, take some new corks which you have previously soaked in water, drive them as tight as possible, have the bottles so full that there may be no vacancy between the cork and milk, then tie them with pack-thread or wire, as you would porter; when you pack them by, put the bottles with their neck down, and bottom upwards.

N. B. When you first cork them, put some straw on the bottom of a boiler, then place your bottles on their bottoms on it, and fill up with cold water, make a fire, and when it begins to boil, take the fire from under the boiler, and let it cool down.

When cool, take them out, and pack as above, in straw, or saw dust. I have frequently kept milk for six months, and it was as fresh as when first bottled.

73.—TO PRESERVE APPLES
FOR THE YEAR ROUND

Put them in casks in layers of dry sand; let the sand be perfectly dry, and each layer being covered keeps them from the air, from moisture, from frost, and from perishing, as the sand absorbs their moisture, which generally perishes them; pippins have often been kept in this manner until mid-summer, and were as fresh then as when put in.

74.—TO LOOSEN STOPPERS OF
DECANTERS THAT ARE CONGEALED

Put two or three drops of sweet oil round the stopper close to the mouth of the decanter, then lay it a little distance from the fire, with the mouth of the bottle towards the heat, when the decanter gets warm, and the oil soaked in, take a piece of wood with a thick cloth wrapped around the heavy end of it for this purpose, then strike at one side, and then at the other, but not very hard, by this process you will soon take it out; or instead of putting the decanters before the fire, put them in some boiling water, and pound them as above.

75.—TAKING STAINS OUT OF
BLACK CLOTH, CRAPE, OR SILK

Boil a large handful of fig leaves in two quarts of rain or soft water, until reduced to one pint, then squeeze the leaves, and put the liquor into a bottle, cork it tight. The way to apply this is to rub the article with a piece of sponge dipped in the liquor, and the stain will immediately disappear.

76.—TO KNOW WHETHER A BED IS DAMP OR NOT, WHEN TRAVELLING

After the bed is warmed, put a glass tumbler between the sheets, and if the bed is damp, the tumbler will show drops of wet on the inside. This rule ought to be properly attended to, and especially when you are travelling with a family, as it is your duty to be as attentive to them as possible.

77.—TO MAKE THE BEST GINGER BEER

Take one ounce of powdered ginger, half an ounce of cream tartar, one large lemon cut in slices, two pounds of loaf sugar, and one gallon of soft water, let them be well mixed together, let them simmer over the fire for half an hour, then put in one table-spoonful of yeast, and let it stand to ferment, and when done, bottle it and tie the corks with twine, put it in a cool place, and it will be fit for use in five or six days. This is delicious in hot weather.

78.—TO MAKE EXCELLENT SPRUCE BEER

Take eight gallons of boiling water, add to it eight gallons of cold, mix with this sixteen pounds of molasses, and six table-spoonsful of best essence of spruce, and half a pint of good yeast; keep your keg in a temperate place, let the bung-hole remain open for two days, after which stop it up tight, or bottle it off. It will be fit for use in a few days; you can make any quantity you choose, by either adding or diminishing the ingredients, &c.

79.—TO MAKE A BEAUTIFUL FLAVOURED PUNCH

Take one dessert-spoonful of acid salt of lemon, half a pound of good white sugar, two quarts of real boiling water, one pint of

Jamaica rum, and half a pint of brandy, add some lemon peel or some essence of lemon, if agreeable, four drops of the essence is enough; then pour it from one pitcher to another twice or thrice to mix it well. This will be a most delicious and fine flavoured punch.

80.—TO CEMENT ANY KIND OF BROKEN GLASS

Take some isinglass, dissolve it in a sufficient quantity of spirits of wine, this will form a transparent glue that will unite glass so that the fracture will scarcely be perceived; be very careful in handling the spirits of wine, for fear that it might boil into the fire, for this would be very dangerous.

81.—A BLACK VARNISH FOR STRAW OR CHIP HATS

Take half an ounce of best black varnish sealing wax, rectified spirits of wine two ounces, powder the sealing wax and put it into a four ounce phial, digest them in a sand heat, or near a fire, until the wax is quite dissolved; lay it on the hat when warm, with a soft paint brush, be careful to lay it on very even. This gives straw or chip hats a fine stiffness and a beautiful glaze, which will resist all wet and storm.

82.—BLACKING FOR HARNESS THAT WILL NOT INJURE THE LEATHER

Take two pounds of hog's fat, one pound of best ivory black, mix them well together, then add spirits of turpentine to bring it to the consistence of paint, apply it on your harness with a brush, in the same manner as blacking a boot, then polish off with another, and it will produce a beautiful jet black, and is a great preservation to the leather; almost all other compositions are injurious.

83.—TO MAKE A STRONG PASTE FOR PAPER

Take two table-spoonsful of flour, stir it well together to make it free from lumps, then add as much strong beer as will make it to a due consistency; boil slow for twenty minutes, let it be cold before you use it.

N. B. Common paste may be made of flour, water, and a little alum. To preserve paste from souring, rats, &c. add a little spirits of turpentine.

84.—A WATER THAT GILDS
COPPER AND BRONZE

Dissolve equal quantities of green vitriol and ammoniac salt, in good double distilled vinegar, then evaporate the vinegar and put it in the retort to distil; if in the product of your distillation you steep your metal, and after you have polished and made hot, it will come out perfectly well gilt.

85.—A WASH FOR GOLD, SILVER, SILK, OR ANY
OTHER KIND OF EMBROIDERY
OR STUFF WHATEVER

Take bullock's galls one pound, soft soap and honey of each three ounces. Florentine orris of the same quantity, in subtile powder, put all into a glass or china vessel, in which mix well to a paste, and let it be exposed to the heat of the sun for the space of twelve days; when you want to use it, make an infusion of bran boiled in soft water, and strained through a cloth, then smear the work above with the paste, wherever it is soiled or dirty, and wash afterwards in this bran water, still renewing the above, until there is no alteration in its colour, then wipe the places with a clean cloth, and wrap them in a clean napkin and place in the sun to dry; after which you may pass it through the polish press and the work will appear as when new.

86.—TO MAKE IRON AS BEAUTIFUL AND WHITE AS SILVER

Take ammoniac salt and quick lime in equal quantities, mix them well together, and dilute them in equal quantities of soft cold water, then take whatever piece of iron that you choose to make bright, heat it red hot, then steep it in the liquor prepared, and it will come out as beautiful and bright as silver.

87.—TO PRESERVE FURS OR WOOLLEN CLOTHES FROM MOTHS

Let the former be combed often while in use, and the latter be brushed and shaken, and when not wanted let them be dried and cool, then among them mix bitter apples, which you can buy at the apothecaries, put them in small muslin bags, and carefully wrap them in several folds of linen, turning them up carefully at the ends and edges; put them by in a dry place.

88.—TO DYE GLOVES TO LOOK LIKE YORK TAN

Put into half or one pint of soft water, half an ounce of best saffron, let the water be boiling, let this infuse all night; the next morning wet the gloves well and even all over with a brush, you must sew up the tops to prevent the colour from getting inside; if the first colour don't suit, give them another coat.

89.—TO CURE THOSE THAT ARE GIVEN TO DRINK

Put, in a sufficient quantity of rum, brandy, gin, or whatever liquor the person is in the habit of drinking, three large live eels, which leave until quite dead, give this liquor unawares to those you wish to reform, and they will get so disgusted against it, that, though they formerly liked it, they will now have quite an aversion to it afterwards; this I have seen tried and have the good effect on the person who drank it.

90.—TO PREVENT THE BREATH FROM SMELLING AFTER DRINK

Chew a bit of the root of iris-troglotida, and no person can discover by your breath whether you have been drinking or not.

91.—A WASH TO GIVE LUSTRE TO THE FACE

Infuse half a pound of wheat bran in one quart of best white wine vinegar, for the space of four hours; add to it the yolks of five eggs well beaten, and two grains of ambergris, distil the whole, and bottle it for use; cork it very close, let it stand for fourteen days before use; this must be applied at night and in the morning, mixed in soft water.

92.—A WASH FOR THE HAIR MOST SUPERB

Beat up the yolks of six eggs into a froth, and with this anoint the head well over, rub it well into the roots of the hair, leave it on until dry, then take equal quantities of rum and rose water, and wash the head well over, this is a beautiful cleanser and brightener to the head and hair; this should be applied in the morning.

93.—EXCELLENT PASTE FOR THE SKIN

This can be highly recommended in cases when the skin gets too loosely attached to the muscles; boil the whites of eggs in rose water, add to this a sufficiently good quantity of alum in fine powder, beat all well up together, to form a paste; this will give a great firmness to the skin when properly applied.

94.—A BEAUTIFUL CORN POULTICE, BY R. R. THE AUTHOR

Take equal parts of roasted onions and soft soap, beat them well up together, and apply it hot to the corn; this I have known to assuage the raging pain of a corn.

95.—TO MAKE THE BEST CORN PLASTER, BY J. W.

Take one ounce of Venice turpentine, half an ounce of red lead, one ounce of frankincense, half a pound of white rosin, one pint of Florence oil; boil these in a pipkin over a slow fire, stir with a stick until they turn black, then turn it out to harden, this must be applied by spreading it on a piece of leather, that is oiled all over, then put it on the corn, wearing it constantly, and in a short time it will eradicate the corn.

96.—A SAFE LIQUID TO TURN RED HAIR BLACK

Take black lead finely powdered, one ounce, ebony shavings one ounce; mix these ingredients in one pint of soft water, boil for one hour; let it stand until fine, then bottle it for use. To apply this, wet the comb often, and the hair must be frequently combed; if a fine glossy black be required, you must add two ounces of camphor.

97.—TO REFINE CIDER, FOR ONE BARREL

Take one pint of brandy, four ounces of rock alum, the whites of six eggs, half a pint of coarse sand, and two pounds of coarse sugar.

98.—TO CLARIFY STRONG OR TABLE BEER

Take a piece of chalk as big as a common tumbler glass, and cut it in two pieces of equal size, put it into your beer through the bung hole, this will answer for one barrel, and will cause the liquor to foment and become perfectly clear and fine.

99.—A CHEAP AND WHOLESOME BEER

Boil two ounces of hops, two ounces of pounded ginger, eight pounds of molasses, in four gallons of water, when it is cooled down to milk warm, add some yeast to ferment it. This makes a very wholesome and agreeable beer, and is not only cheaper, but will keep much longer than common beer.

100.—EXCELLENT JUMBLE BEER

Take four table-spoonsful of ground ginger, one quart of molasses, ten gallons of water. N. B. First mix the ingredients in a little warm water, then add the whole complement of water, and shake it briskly, and in eight hours it will be sufficiently fermented, and is a wholesome and pleasant beer.

101.—TO MAKE GINGER BEER, FOR TEN GALLONS

Take ten gallons of water, one quart of molasses, ten good lemons cut in slices, ten ounces of bruised ginger, the whites of eight eggs well beaten, mix all well together, boil it for half an hour, skim it before it boils, add half an ounce of isinglass, and one pint of yeast; add the yeast when milk warm, leave the bung open for it to ferment; when done, stop it tight to keep, or you may bottle it after six days. You must tie the corks with twine, and put it in a cool place.

102.—A WASH TO GIVE A BRILLIANT LUSTRE TO PLATE

Take one quart of rain or soft water, dissolve in it four ounces of good alum, when the alum is perfectly dissolved take it off the coals and skim it very clean, then bottle it and cork it close. When you want to use it, dip a soft sponge into some of this liquor, which you must pour out into a bowl, and mix with it a little soft soap, say a teaspoonful; rub it well and even over your plate, dry with warm towels, and polish with leather.

103.—WATER PROOF VARNISH OF THE BEST QUALITY

Take linseed oil of the best quality, put any quantity you please into a well glazed pipkin over some red hot charcoal, in a chafingdish, then add to the oil, when warming, the fourth part of its weight in fine powder of rosin, dissolve them well together; when you want to try it, take a little of the oil, and if it draws like thread, you may take it off the fire; if it prove too thin, add some more rosin, and continue to boil; when it comes as it should be, take whatever article that you have to varnish, and when finished, put it in the sun to dry, or put it before the fire, as this varnish will not dry itself.

104.—CHINESE VARNISH FOR MINIATURE PAINTING

Take one ounce of white karabe or amber, and one drachm of camphor reduced into subtile powder, put them into a matrass with five ounces of spirits of wine, and put it in the sun for twelve or fourteen days in the hottest weather, after which place the matrass on hot ashes for the space of one hour, then strain it through a linen cloth, and bottle and cork it tight for use.

105.—TO MAKE BOTTLE CEMENT

Half a pound of black rosin, same quantity of red sealing wax, quarter of an ounce of bees wax, melted in an earthen or iron pot; when it froths up, before all is melted and likely to boil over, stir it with a tallow candle, which will settle the froth till all is melted and fit for use.

I have now set down all the receipts that I thought were the best. I might have given a hundred more, for I have hundreds written off, but all these that I have put down I have tried myself, and find them all genuine; I shall now give you some directions for putting dishes, &c. on table.

DIRECTIONS FOR PUTTING DISHES ON TABLE

Soup, broth, or fish, should always be set at the head of the table; if none of these, a boiled dish goes to the head, where there is both boiled and roasted.

If but one principal dish, it goes to the head of the table.

If three, the principal one to the head, and the two smallest to stand opposite each other, near the foot.

If four, the biggest to the head, and the next biggest to the foot, and the two smallest dishes on the sides.

If five, you are to put the smallest in the middle, the other four opposite.

If six, you are to put the top and bottom as before, the two small ones opposite for side dishes.

If seven, you are to put three dishes down the middle of the table, and four others opposite to each other round the centre dish.

If eight, put four dishes down the middle, and the remaining four two on each side, at equal distances.

If nine dishes, put them in three equal lines, observing to put the proper dishes at the head and bottom of the table.

If ten dishes, put four down the centre, one at each corner, and one on each side, opposite to the vacancy between two central dishes; or four down the middle, and three on each side; each opposite to the vacancy of the middle dishes.

If twelve dishes, place them in three rows of four each; or six down the middle, and three at equal distances on each side.

NOTE.—If more than the above number of dishes are required, the manner of laying them on the table must in a great measure depend on the taste of the dresser.

Desserts are placed in same manner;—if you have an ornamental frame for desserts, or a bouquet, or any other ornament, for your dinner-table, invariably place them in the middle of the table.

THE UNIFORM POSITION TO PLACE DIFFERENT JOINTS, &c. ON TABLE

Let the heads of fish always be placed to the left hand of the carver; likewise the heads of hares, rabbits, and roasting pigs in like manner. An aitch bone of beef, let the silver skewer, which is generally put into it when for a party dish, be placed towards the left hand of the carver. A quarter of lamb, let the thin part be put from the carver, towards the centre of the table, with the neck end to the left of the carver. A shoulder and leg of mutton should be placed with the shank of either to the left hand of the carver, unless your mistress or master otherwise order it. Turkies, geese, ducks, and fowls, are to be placed with the heads towards the right hand of the carver. Likewise woodcocks, snipes, partridges, and all sorts of wild fowls are to be placed in the like manner as above, because they are much easier to carve in this manner.

There are some people that will choose to have the heads of turkies, geese, and ducks, put towards their left hand, as they may then be able to come at the stuffing more handily.

In the sirloin of beef, let the thick boney end be placed to the left hand of the carver. The saddle or loin of mutton, the rump end to be placed in like manner.

In many large dishes that are for head and foot, there is a place for the gravy in one end of them; observe always to put this end to the right hand of the carver, observing likewise not to forget the large gravy spoon.

All these rules you should observe, and pay great attention to them, for in the course of time you will find out how much trouble and difficulty there is in turning a large dish round, after the company have sat down, besides, it looks careless in the servant.

DIRECTIONS FOR CARVING

This is a part of duty, which a house servant is seldom called upon to perform; but, in case of the sickness of his employers, it is possible he may be ordered occasionally on this business of the table; to be found incompetent or awkward in such emergency would be mortifying to both master and servant, I have therefore, my young friends, selected a few observations on this delicate and important art for your information. A complete and full knowledge of the business would do you no harm; depend upon it you cannot learn too much of every thing in the least connected with service; if you should never be called upon to exercise your skill at your employer's table, you will perhaps daily or frequently find use for your talents at the servants' table, or, when you quit service and have a family of your own; and neatness and skill are requisite in every thing you undertake, and in every station, whether for your employers, or for your equals. I would not have you intrusive, which would be worse than ignorance, but let your 'light be hid under a bushel,' always ready for modest use, if required. I shall now give you directions for carving several kinds of meat, fish, fowls, &c.

The carving-knife should be light, yet of a sufficient size, and the edge very keen. In using it, no great personal strength is requisite, as constant practice will render it an easy task to carve the most difficult articles, more depending on address than force; but, in order to prevent trouble, the joints of mutton, veal, lamb, &c. should be divided by the butcher, when they may be easily cut through, and fine slices of meat taken off from between every two bones.

The more fleshy joints are to be cut in smooth slices, neatly done; and in joints of beef and mutton, the knife should always be passed down the bone by those who wish to carve with propriety, and great attention should be paid to help every person to a portion of the best parts. Fish should be carefully helped, because if the flakes are broken, the beauty of it is entirely lost, for which reason a proper fish slice should be used, and observe to send a part of the roe, liver, &c. to each individual. The heads of cod, salmon, carp, the fins of turbot, and sounds of cod, are esteemed as delicacies, and, of course some should be sent to each person in company, which denotes an attentive degree of politeness towards your guests. In carving ducks, geese, turkeys, or wild fowl, you should cut the slices down from pinion to pinion, without making wings, by which you will gain more prime pieces; but you need only do this when your party is large.

A COD'S HEAD

Fish is easily carved. The dish now under consideration, in its proper season, is esteemed a delicacy; when served up, it should be cut with a fish-slice, and it should be remembered that the parts about the back-bone and the shoulders are generally accounted the best. Cut a piece quite off down to the bone, observing with each piece to help a part of the sound. There are several delicate parts about the head; the jelly part lies about the jaw bone, and is by some esteemed very fine, and the firm parts will be found within the head.

ROUND OF BEEF

This valuable and excellent dish must be cut in thin slices, and very smooth with a sharp knife, observing to help every person to a portion of the fat, also cut in thin smooth slices, as nothing has a worse appearance than fat when hacked. Observe, also, that a thick slice should be cut off the meat, before you begin to help your friends, as the boiling water renders the outside vapid, and of course unfit for your guests.

EDGE-BONE OF BEEF

Take off a slice three quarters of an inch thick, all the length, and then help your guests; the soft marrow-like fat is situated at the back of the bone below, the solid fat will be duly portioned from its situation with each slice you cut. The skewer with which the meat is held together while boiling, should be removed before the meat is brought to table, as nothing can be more unpleasant than to meet with a skewer when carving; but as some articles require one to be left in, a silver skewer should be invariably employed for that purpose.

SIRLOIN OF BEEF

You may begin carving a sirloin of beef either at the end, or by cutting into the middle; cut your slices close down to the bone, and let them be thin, observing to give some of the soft fat with each slice. Many persons prefer the outside; it is therefore a point of politeness to enquire which they will take.

FILLET OF VEAL

The bone of this piece being taken out, renders the helping of it very easy. Many persons prefer the outside,—ask this; and if so, help them to it, otherwise cut it off, and then continue to take off thin smooth slices; observing to take from the flap, into which you must cut deep, a portion of stuffing to every slice, as likewise a small bit of fat. Lemon should always be served with this joint.

BREAST OF VEAL

Is composed of two parts, the ribs and brisket, the latter is thickest, and is composed of gristles, the division of which you may easily discern, at which part you must enter your knife, and cut through it, which will separate the two parts, then proceed to help your guests to whatever part they chance to prefer.

CALF'S HEAD

Cut out slices, observing to pass your knife close into the bone; at the thick part of the neck is situated the throat, sweet-bread, which you should carve a slice of with the other part, that your guests may have a portion of each. If the eye is preferred, which is frequently the case, take it out, cut it in two, send one half to the person who prefers it, and on removing the jaw-bone, some lean will be found, if required. The palate, generally esteemed a peculiar delicacy, is situated under the head: this should be divided into small portions, and a part helped to each person.

SHOULDER OF MUTTON

Cut into the bone; the prime part of the fat lies in the outer edge, and must be thinly and smoothly sliced; when your company is large, and it becomes necessary to have more meat than can be cut as above directed, some very fine slices may be cut out on each side of the blade bone, but observe, the blade bone cannot be cut across.

LEG OF MUTTON

Wether mutton is esteemed the best, and may be known by a lump of fat at the edge of the broadest part, the slices are situated in the centre; when you carve, put your knife in there, and cut thin smooth slices, and, as the outside is rarely fat enough, cut some from the side of the broad end in neat slices. Some persons prefer the knuckle, the question should therefore be always asked; on the back of the leg there are several fine slices, for which purpose turn it up, and cut the meat out lengthways. The cramp-bone is generally esteemed a delicacy; to cut it out, take hold of the shank with your left hand, and cut down to the thigh bone, then pass the knife under the cramp bone.

A FORE-QUARTER OF LAMB

Divide the shoulder from the breast and ribs, by passing the knife under, observing not to cut the meat too much off the bones. When the lamb is large, put the shoulder in another dish, and squeeze half a lemon over it, and the same over the breast and ribs, with a little pepper and salt, then divide the grisly part from the ribs, and help agreeably to the taste of your guests.

HAUNCH OF VENISON

Pass your knife down to the bone, which will let out the gravy, then turn the broadest end of the joint towards you, and put in your knife, cutting as deep as you can to the end of the haunch; let your slices be thin and smooth, the fat, which is always esteemed, to each person; you will find most fat on the left side, which, with the gravy, must be properly divided among your guests.

HAUNCH OF MUTTON

Consists of a leg and a part of the loin, cut so as to resemble a haunch of venison, and must be carved in the same manner.

SADDLE OF MUTTON

Take your slices from the tail to the end, commencing close to the back bone; let them be long, thin, and smooth; a portion of fat to each slice must be taken from the sides.

ROAST PIG

This is generally divided by the cook before it is served up. You must first divide the shoulder from the body on one side, and then the leg, the ribs are next to be separated in two or three parts, and an ear or jaw presented with them, together with a sufficiency of proper sauce. The ribs are commonly thought to be the finest part; but as this must depend on taste, the question should be asked.

HAM

The best method of helping ham is to begin in the middle by cutting long slices through the thick fat. When made use of for pies, the meat should be cut from the under side, after taking off a thick slice.

GOOSE

Separate the apron, and pour a glass of port wine into the body, and a little ready mixed mustard, then cut the whole breast in long slices, but remove them only as you help them; separate the leg from the body by putting the fork into the small end of the bone, pressing it to the body, and having passed the knife, turn the leg back. To take off the wing, put your fork into the small end of the pinion, and press it close to the body; then put in the knife, and divide the joint down. However, practice can alone render persons expert at this; when you have thus taken off the leg and wing on one side, do the same by the other, if it be necessary, which will not be the case unless your company is large; by the wing there are two side bones, which may be taken off, as may the back and lower side bones, but the breast and the thighs, divided from the drum-sticks, afford the finest and most delicious pieces.

FOWLS

The legs of a boiled fowl are bent inwards, and tucked in the belly; but the skewers must be removed before it is sent to table. To carve a fowl, take it on your plate, and as you separate the joints, place them on the dish; cut the wing off, observing only to divide the joint with your knife; then lift the pinion with your fork and draw the wings towards the legs which will separate the fleshy part more effectually than cutting it; to separate the leg, slip the knife between the leg and body, and cut the bone; then, with the fork, turn the leg back, and the joint will give way; when the wings and legs are in this manner removed, take off the merry-thought, and the neck bones; the next thing is to divide the breast from the body, by cutting through the tender ribs, close to the breast, entirely down to the tail; then lay the back upwards, put your knife into the bone half ways from the neck to the rump, and on raising the lower end, it will readily separate. The breast and wings are the most delicate parts; however, the best way is to consult the taste of your guests, by asking which part they prefer.

PARTRIDGE

The skewers must be taken out before it is sent to table, and it is then to be carved in the same manner as a fowl. The wings, breast, and merry-thought, are the primest parts.

PIGEONS

Should be divided right in halves, either lengthways or across, and half helped to each person.

In respect to carving, written directions must always fail without constant practice, as that can alone give the necessary facility.

GOING TO MARKET

Your employer will generally attend to going to market, to suit himself; but your experience, if you should be called upon to do this duty, is of the utmost consequence. It is impossible to give you particular directions for all kinds of articles for the table; in all cases observation and experience only can supply you with these to any degree of perfection. I shall merely set down some of the principal means of judging of the freshness or goodness of provisions, in the choice of poultry, &c. Beef, veal, pork, mutton, and vegetables, you all are generally competent of purchasing.

LAMB

In a fore-quarter of lamb mind the neck vein: if it be an azure blue, it is new and good; but if green or yellow, it is near tainting if not tainted already. In the hind quarter, smell under the kidney, and try the knuckle; if you meet with a faint scent, and the knuckle be limber, it is stale killed. For a lamb's head, mind the eyes; if sunk or wrinkled, it is stale; if plump and lively, it is new and sweet.

VEAL

If the bloody vein in the shoulder looks blue, or of a bright red, it is new killed; but if black, green, or yellow, it is flabby and stale; if wrapped in wet cloths, smell whether it be musty or not. For the loin first taints under the kidney; and the flesh, if stale killed, will be soft and slimy.

The breast and neck taints first at the upper end, and you will perceive a dusky, yellow, or green appearance; and the sweetbread on the breast will be clammy, otherwise it is fresh and good. The leg is known to be new by the stiffness of the joint; if limber and the flesh seems clammy, and has green or yellow specks, it is stale. The head is known as the lamb's.

The flesh of a bull-calf is more red and firm than that of a cow-calf, and the fat more hard curdled.

MUTTON

If it be young, the flesh will pinch tender; if old, it will wrinkle and remain so: if young, the fat will easily part from the lean; if old, it will stick by strings and skins: if ram-mutton, the fat feels spungy, the flesh close-grained and tough, not rising again when dented; if ewe-mutton, the flesh is paler than wether mutton, a close grain and easily parting. If there be a rot, the flesh will be pale, and the fat a faint white inclining to yellow, and the flesh will be loose at the bone. If you squeeze it hard, some drops of water will stand up like sweat.

As to the newness and staleness, the same is to be observed as in lamb.

BEEF

If it be right ox-beef, it will have an open grain; if young, a tender and oily smoothness; if rough and spongy, it is old, or inclined to be so, except the neck, brisket, and such parts as are very fibrous, which in young meat will be more rough than other parts.

A carnation, pleasant colour, betokens good meat: the suet a curious white; yellow is not good. Cow-beef is less bound and closer grained than ox, the fat whiter, but the lean somewhat paler; if young, the dent made with the finger will rise again in a little time.

Bull-beef is close grained, deep dusky red, tough in pinching, the fat skinny, hard, and has a rammish rank smell; and for newness, and staleness, this flesh brought fresh has but few signs, the more material is its clamminess, and the rest your smell will inform you. If it be bruised, these places will look more dusky or blacker than the rest.

PORK

If young, the lean will break in pinching between the fingers; and if you nip the skin with your nails, it will make a dent; also if the fat be soft and pulpy, like lard: if the lean be tough, and the fat flabby and spongy, feeling rough, it is old, especially if the rind be stubborn, and you cannot nip it with your nails.

If a boar, though young, or a hog gelded at full growth, the flesh will be hard, tough, red, and rammish of smell; the fat skinny and hard; the skin thick and rough, and pinched up, will immediately fall again.

As for old or new killed, try the legs, hands, and springs, by putting the finger under the bone that comes out; if it be tainted, you will there find it by smelling the finger; besides the skin will be sweaty and clammy when stale, but cool and smooth when new.

If you find little kernels in the fat of the pork, like hail-shot, it is measly, and dangerous to be eaten.

BRAWN

Brawn is known to be old or young by the extraordinary or moderate thickness of the rind; the thick is old, moderate young. If the rind and fat be tender, it is not boar brawn but barrow or sow.

VENISON

Try the haunches or shoulders under the bones that come out with your finger or knife, and as the scent is sweet or rank, it is new or stale; and the like of the sides in the fleshy parts; if tainted, they will look green in some places, or more than ordinary black. Look on the hoofs, and if the clefts are very wide and rough, it is old; if close and smooth it is young.

HAMS AND BACON

Put a knife under the bone that sticks out of the ham, and if it comes out in a manner clean, and has a curious flavour, it is sweet; if much smeared and dulled, it is tainted or rusted.

Gammons are tried the same way, and for other parts, try the fat; if it be white, oily in feeling, does not break or crumb, it is good; but if the contrary, and the lean has the little streaks of yellow, it is rusty, or will soon be so.

HARE, LEVERET, OR RABBIT

Hare will be white and stiff, if new and clean killed: if stale, the flesh black in most parts, and the body limber: if the cleft in her lips spread much, and her claws wide and ragged, she is old; the contrary young: if young, the ears will tare like brown paper; if old, dry and tough. To know a true leveret, feel on the foreleg, near the foot, and if there is a small bone or knob, it is right; if not it is a hare; for the rest observe as in a hare. A rabbit, if stale, will be limber and slimy; if new, white and stiff: if old, her claws are long and rough, the wool mottled with grey hairs; if young, claws and wool smooth.

BUTTER

When you buy butter, trust not to that which will be given you, but try in the middle, and if your smell and taste be good, you cannot be deceived.

CHEESE

Cheese is to be chosen by its moist and smooth coat; if old cheese be rough coated, rugged, or dry at top, beware of little worms or mites; if it be over full of holes, moist or spongy, it is subject to mites; if soft or perished places appear on the outside, try how deep it goes, the greater part may be hid.

EGGS

Hold the great end to your tongue; if it feels warm it is new; if cold, bad; and so in proportion to the heat or cold, is the goodness of the egg. Another way to know, is to put the egg in a pan of cold water, the fresher the egg, the sooner it will fall to the bottom; if rotten, it will swim at the top. This is a sure way not to be deceived. Sound eggs may be also known by holding them between the eye and a lighted candle, or the sun. As to the keeping of them, pitch them all with the small end downwards in fine wood ashes, turning them once a week end-ways, and they will keep some months.

HOW TO CHOOSE POULTRY

CAPONS

If it be young, his spurs are short, and his legs smooth: if a true capon, a fat vein on the side of his breast, the comb pale, and a thick belly and rump: if new, he will have a hard close vent: if stale, a loose open vent.

A COCK OR HEN TURKEY, TURKEY POULTS

If the cock be young, his legs will be black and smooth, and his spurs short; if stale, his eyes will be sunk in his head, and the feet dry; if new, the eyes lively, and feet limber. Observe the like by the hens; and moreover, if she be with egg, she will have a soft open vent; if not, a hard close vent. Turkey poults are known the same, their age cannot deceive you.

COCK, HEN, &C.

If young, his spurs are short and dubbed; but take particular notice they are not pared or scraped: if old, he will have an open vent; but if new, a close hard vent. And so of a hen for newness or staleness; if old, her legs and comb are rough; if young, smooth.

A TAME, WILD, AND BRAN GOOSE

If the bill be yellow, and she has but a few hairs, she is young, but if full of hairs, and the bill and foot red, she is old; if new, limber-footed; if stale, dry-footed. And so of a wild bran goose.

WILD AND TAME DUCKS

The duck, when fat, is hard and thick on the belly; if not, thin and lean; if new, limber-footed; if stale, dry-footed. A true wild duck has a red foot, smaller than the tame one.

PARTRIDGE, COCK AND HEN

The bill white, and the legs blue, show age; for if young, the bill is black, and the legs yellow; if new, a fast vent; if stale, a green and open one. If full crops, and they have fed on green food, they may taint there; for this, smell the mouth.

WOODCOCK AND SNIPE

The woodcock, if fat, is thick and hard; if new, limber-footed; when stale, dry-footed; or if their noses are slimy, and their throats muddy and moorish, they are not good. A snipe, if fat, has a fat vein on the side under the wing, and in the vent feels thick. For the rest, like the woodcock.

DOVES AND PIGEONS

To know the turtle-dove, look for a blue ring round his neck, and the rest mostly white.

The pigeon is bigger; and the ring-dove is less than the pigeon. The dove-house pigeons, when old, are red-legged; if new and fat, they will feel full and fat in the vent, and are limber-footed; but if stale, a flabby and green vent.

So the green or grey plover, fieldfare, blackbird, thrush, larks, &c.

HOW TO CHOOSE FISH

SALMON, PIKE, TRENT, CARP, TENCH, GRAILING, BARBEL, CHUB, RUFF, EEL, WHITING, SMELT, SHAD, &C.

All these are known to be new or stale by the colour of their gills, their easiness or hardness to open, the hanging or keeping up of the fins, the standing out or sinking of the eyes, and by smelling the gills.

TURBOT

He is chosen by his thickness and plumpness; and if his belly be of a cream colour, he must spend well; but if thin, and his belly of a bluish white, he will eat very loose.

COD AND CODLING

Choose by his thickness towards the head, and the whiteness of his flesh when it is cut: and so of a codling.

STURGEON

If it cuts without crumbling, and the veins and gristles give a true blue where they appear, and the flesh a perfect white, then conclude it to be good.

FRESH HERRINGS AND MACKEREL

If their gills are of a lively shining redness, their eyes stand full, and the fish is stiff, then they are new; but if dusky and faded, or sinking and wrinkled, and tails limber, they are stale.

LOBSTERS

Choose by their weight; the heaviest are best, if no water be in them; if new, the tail will pull smart, like a spring; if full, the middle of the tail will be full of hard, or red-skinned meat. A cock lobster is known by the narrow back part of the tail, and the two uppermost fins within his tail are stiff and hard; but the hen is soft, and the back of her tail broader.

PLAICE AND FLOUNDERS

If they are stiff, and their eyes be not sunk or look dull, they are new; the contrary when stale. The best sort of plaice look blue on the belly.

A FEW OBSERVATIONS TO COOKS, &c.

Thus far, Joseph and David, I have addressed myself to you, and might here conclude my observations; but, as this book may fall into the hands not only of those who call themselves house servants, but of the cook, and every other attendant on large or small families, I have appended a few observations addressed to servants generally, but more especially to the cook, and assistant cook; and, that I might not be thought guilty of presumption, in teaching what it may be thought I may not perfectly understand myself, or, as the old saying is, 'swim beyond my depth,' I shall quote this important part of the work from a most approved author, of whose knowledge on these points there can be no doubt. Some things mentioned may not particularly apply to the case in hand; but generally speaking, the remarks and advice are such as should be read by every individual in every kitchen of every great family.

On your first coming into a family,, lose no time in immediately getting into the good graces of your fellow-servants, that you may learn from them the customs of the kitchen, and the various rules and orders of the house.

Take care to be on good terms with the servant who waits at table; you may make use of him as your centinel to inform you how your work has pleased in the parlour, and by his report you may be enabled in some measure to rectify any mistake: but request the favour of an interview with your master or mistress,—depend as little as possible on second-hand opinions—judge of your employers from your own observations, and their behaviour to you, not from any idle reports from the other servants, who, if your master or mistress inadvertently drop a word in your praise—will immediately take alarm, and fearing your being more in favour than themselves, will seldom stick at trifles to prevent it, by pretending to take a prodigious liking to you, and poisoning your mind in such a manner as to destroy all your confidence, &c. in your employers, and if they do not immediately succeed in worrying you away—will take care that you have no comfort while you stay.

If you are a good cook, and have tolerably fair play, you will soon become a favourite domestic, if your master is a man of taste; but never boast of his approbation, for in proportion as you think you rise in his estimation—you will excite all the tricks that envy, hatred, and malice, and all uncharitableness, can suggest to your fellow-servants; every one of whom, if less diligent, or less favoured than yourself will be your enemy.

While we warn you against making others your enemy, we must caution you also to take care that you do not yourself become your own and greatest enemy. 'Favourites are never in greater danger of falling, than when in the greatest favour,' which often begets a careless inattention to the commands of their employers, and insolent overbearance to their equals, a gradual neglect of duty, and a corresponding forfeiture of that regard which can only be preserved by the means which created it.

If your employers are so pleased with your conduct as to treat you as a friend rather than a servant, do not let their kindness excite your self-conceit, so as to make you for a moment forget you are one. Condescension even to a proverb produces contempt in inconsiderate minds—and to such the very means which benevolence takes to cherish attention to duty, becomes the cause of the evil you wished to prevent.

To be an agreeable companion in the kitchen, without compromising your duty to your patrons in the parlour, requires no small portion of good sense and good nature; in a word, you must 'do as you would be done by.'

Act for, and speak of every body, as if they were present.

We hope the culinary student who peruses these pages, will be above adopting the common, mean and base, and ever unsuccessful way of 'holding with the hare, and running with the hounds,'—of currying favour with fellow-servants by flattering them, and ridiculing the mistress when in the kitchen, and then prancing into the parlour and purring about her, and making opportunities to display all the little faults you can find (or invent) that will tell well against those in the kitchen, assuring them, on your return, that they were praised, for whatever you heard them blamed; and so, excite them to run more extremely into any little error, which you think will be most displeasing to their employers, watching an opportunity to pour your poisonous lies into their unsuspecting ears, when there is no third person to bear witness of your inquiry—making your victims believe it is all out of your sincere regard for them—assuring them (as Betty says in the Man of the World)—"That indeed you are no busybody that loves fending nor proving, but hate all tittling and tattling—and gossiping and back-biting," &c. &c.

Depend upon it, if you hear fellow-servants speak disrespectfully of a master or mistress with whom they have lived some time, it is a sure sign that they have some sinister scheme against yourself. If they have not been well treated, why have they stayed?

"There is nothing more detestable than defamation; I have no scruple to rank a slanderer with a murderer or an assassin. Those who assault the reputation of their benefactors, and 'rob you of that which nought enriches them,' would destroy your life, if they could do it with equal impunity."

"If you hope to gain the esteem and respect of others, and the approbation of your own heart, be respectful and faithful to your superiors, obliging and good-natured to your fellow-servants, and charitable to all."

"Let your character be remarkable for industry and moderation; your manners and deportment, for modesty and humility; and your dress distinguished for simplicity, frugality and neatness; if you outshine your companions in finery, you will most inevitably excite their envy, and make them your enemies."

"Do every thing at the proper time."

"Keep every thing in its proper place."

"Use every thing for its proper purpose."

"Never think any part of your business too trifling to be well done."

"Eagerly embrace every opportunity of learning any thing which may be useful to yourself, or of doing any thing which may benefit others."

Do not throw yourself out of a good place for a slight affront. "Come when you are called, and do what you are bid."

Place yourself in your master's situation, and then consider what you would expect from him, if he were in yours.

Although there may be "more places than parish churches," it is not very easy to find many more good ones.

"A rolling stone never gathers moss."

"Honesty is the best policy."

"A still tongue, makes a wise head."

"Saucy answers are highly aggravating, and serve no good purpose."

Let your master or mistress scold ever so much, or be ever so unreasonable; as "a soft answer turneth away wrath,"—so "will silence, or a mild answer, be the best a servant can make."

"If your employers are hasty, and have scolded without reason, bear it patiently; they will soon see their error, and be happy to make you amends. Muttering on leaving the room, or slamming the door after you, is as bad as an impertinent reply; it is, in fact, showing that you would be impertinent if you dared."

"A faithful servant will not only never speak disrespectfully to her employers, but will not hear disrespectful words said of them."

Apply direct to your employers, and beg of them to explain to you, as fully as possible, how they like their victuals dressed, whether much, or little done.

Of what complexion they wish the roasts, of a gold colour, or well browned, and if they like them frothed?

Do they like soups and sauces, thick or thin, or white or brown, clean or full in the mouth? What accompaniments they are partial to?

What flavours they fancy? especially of spice and herbs.

It is impossible that the most accomplished cook can please their palates, till she has learned their particular taste; this, it can hardly be expected, she can hit exactly the first time, however, the hints we have here given, will very much facilitate the ascertainment of this main chance of getting into their favour.

The sense of taste depends much on the health of the individual, and is hardly ever for a single hour in the same state, such is the extremely intimate sympathy between the stomach and the tongue, that in proportion as the former is empty, the latter is acute and sensitive: this is the cause that "good appetite is the best sauce," and that the dish we find relishing and savoury at luncheon, is insipid at dinner, and at supper quite tasteless.

To taste any thing in perfection, the tongue must be moistened, or the substance applied to it contain moisture, the nervous papillæ which constitute this sense are roused to still more lively sensibility by salt, sugar, aromatics, &c.

If the palate becomes dull by repeated tasting, one of the best ways of refreshing it, is to masticate an apple, or to wash your mouth well with milk.

The incessant exercise of tasting, which a cook is obliged to submit to during the education of her tongue, frequently impairs the very faculty she is trying to improve. "'Tis true, 'tis pity, and pity 'tis," (says a grand gourmand,) "'tis true, her too anxious perseverance to penetrate the mysteries of palatics may diminish the *tact*, exhaust the power and destroy the *index*, without which all her labour is in vain."

Therefore, a sagacious cook, instead of idly and wantonly wasting the excitability of her palate, on the sensibility of which, her reputation and fortune depend, when she has ascertained her relative strength of the flavour of the various ingredients she employs, will call in the balance and the measure, to do the ordinary business, and to preserve her organ of taste with the utmost care, that it may be a faithful oracle to refer to, on grand occasions, and new compositions; of these an ingenious cook may form as endless a variety, as a musician with his seven notes, or a painter with his colours.

Receive as the highest testimonies of your employers' regard, whatever observations they make on your work, such admonitions are the most unequivocal proofs of their desire to make you thoroughly understand their taste, and their wish to retain you in their service, or they would not take the trouble to teach you.

Enter into all their plans of economy, and endeavour to make the most of every thing, as well for your own honour as your master's profit; take care that the meat which is to make its appearance again in the parlour, is handsomely cut with a sharp knife, and put on a clean dish, take care of the gravy which is left, it will save many pounds of meat in making sauce for hashes, poultry, and many little dishes.

Many things may be re-dressed, in a different form, from that in which they were first served, and improve the appearance of the table without increasing the expense of it.

The best way to warm cold meat is to sprinkle the joint over with a little salt, put it in a Dutch oven, at some distance before a gentle fire, that it may warm gradually, watch it carefully, and keep turning it till it is quite hot and brown: it will take from twenty minutes to three quarters of an hour, according to its thickness; serve it up with gravy; this is much better than hashing it, and by doing it nicely, a cook will get great credit. Poultry, fried fish, &c. may be re-dressed this way.

Take care of the liquor you have boiled poultry or meat in; in five minutes you may make it into excellent soup. No good housewife has any pretensions to rational economy who boils animal food without converting the broth into some sort of soup.

However highly the uninitiated in the mystery of soup making may elevate the external appendage of his olfactory organ at the mention of "pot liquor," if he tastes, he will be as well pleased with it, as a Frenchman is with "potage à la camerani," of which it is said "a single spoonful will lap the palate in Elysium, and while a drop of it remains on the tongue, each other sense is eclipsed by the voluptuous thrilling of the lingual nerves!"

Broth of fragments.—When you dress a large dinner, you may make good broth or portable soup at very small cost, by taking care of all the trimmings and parings of the meat, game, and poultry you are going to use; wash them well, and put them into a stewpan, with as much cold water as will cover them; set your stewpan on a hot fire; when it boils, take off all the scum, and set it on again to simmer gently; put in two carrots, two turnips, a large onion, three blades of pounded mace, and a head of celery; some mushroom parings will be a great addition. Let it continue to simmer gently four or five hours, strain it through a sieve into a clean basin. This will save a great deal of expense in buying gravy meat.

Have the dust, &c. removed regularly once a fortnight, and have your kitchen chimney swept once a month; many good dinners have been spoiled, and many houses burnt down by the soot falling; the best security against this, is for the cook to have a long birch broom, and every morning brush down all the soot within reach of it. Give notice to your employers when the contents of your coal cellar are diminished.

It will be to little purpose to procure good provisions, without you have proper utensils to prepare them in: the most expert artist cannot perform his work in a perfect manner without proper instruments; you cannot have neat work without nice tools, nor can you dress victuals well without an apparatus appropriate to the work required.

In those houses where the cook enjoys the confidence of her employer so much as to be intrusted with the care of the store-room, which is not very common, she will keep an exact account of every thing as it comes in, and insist upon the weight and price being fixed to every article she purchases, and occasionally will (and it may not be amiss, to jocosely drop a hint to those who supply them, that she does) re-weigh them for her own satisfaction, as well as that of her employer, and will not trust the key of this room to any one; she will also keep an account of every thing she takes from it, and manage with as much consideration and frugality as if it was her own property she was using, endeavouring to disprove the adage, that "plenty makes waste," and remembering that "wilful waste makes woful want."

The honesty of a cook must be above all suspicion: she must obtain, and, (in spite of the numberless temptations, &c. that daily offer to bend her from it,) preserve a character of spotless integrity, and useful industry, remembering that it is the fair price of independence, which all wish for, but none without it can hope for: only a fool or a madman will be so silly or so crazy, as to expect to reap, where he has been too idle to sow.

Very few modern built town-houses have a proper place to preserve provisions in, the best substitute is a hanging-safe, which you may contrive to suspend in an airy situation, and when you order meat, poultry or fish, tell the tradesman when you intend to dress it, he will then have it in his power to serve you with provision that will do him credit, which the finest meat, &c. in the world will never do, unless it has been kept a proper time to be ripe and tender.

If you have a well-ventilated larder, in a shady, dry situation, you may make it still surer, by ordering in your meat and poultry, such a time before you want it as will render it tender, which the finest meat cannot be, unless hung a proper time, according to the season and nature of the meat, &c. but always as "les bons hommes de bouche de France," say it is "assez mortifée."

Permitting this process to proceed to a certain degree, renders meat much more easy of solution in the stomach, and for those whose digestive faculties are delicate, is of the utmost importance that it be attended to with the greatest nicety, for the most consummate skill in the culinary preparation of it, will not compensate the want of attention to this. Meat that is thoroughly roasted, or boiled, eats much shorter and tenderer, and is in proportion more digestible, than that which is under done.

To encourage the best performance of the machinery of mastication, the cook must take care that her dinner is not only well cooked, but that each dish be sent to table with its proper accompaniments in the neatest and most elegant manner.

Remember that to excite the good opinion of the eye is the first step towards awakening the appetite.

Decoration is much more rationally employed in rendering a plain wholesome nutritious dish inviting, than in the elaborate embellishments which are crowded about trifles and custards.

Endeavour to avoid over-dressing roasts and boils, &c. and over-seasoning soups and sauces, with salt, pepper, &c. it is a fault which cannot be mended.

If your roasts, &c. are a little under-done; with the assistance of the stewpan, the gridiron, or the Dutch oven, you may soon rectify the mistake made with the spit or the pot.

If over-done, the best juices of the meat are evaporated, it will serve merely to distend the stomach, and if the sensation of hunger be removed, it is at the price of an indigestion.

The chief business of cookery, is to render food easy of digestion, and to facilitate nutrition. This is most completely accomplished by plain cookery in perfection, i.e. neither over nor under-done.

With all your care, you will not get credit by cooking to perfection, if more than one dish goes to table at a time.

To be eaten in perfection, the interval between meat being taken out of the stewpan, and its being put into the mouth, must be short as possible: but ceremony, that most formidable enemy to good cheer, too often decrees it otherwise, and the guests seldom get a bit of an "entremet," till it is half cold. So much time is often lost in putting every thing in applepie order, that long before dinner is announced, all becomes lukewarm, and, to complete the mortification of the grand gourmand, his meat is put on a sheet of ice in the shape of a plate, which instantly converts the gravy into jelly, and the fat into a something which puzzles his teeth and the roof of his mouth as much as if he had birdlime to masticate: a complete meat-skreen will answer the purpose of a hot closet, plate-warmer, &c.

Never undertake more work than you are quite certain you can do well: and if you are ordered to prepare a large dinner than you think you can send up with ease and neatness, or to dress any dish you are unacquainted with, rather than run any risk of spoiling any thing, (for by one fault, you may perhaps lose all your credit) request your employer to let you have some help. They will acquit you for pleading guilty of inability, but if you make an attempt, and fail, they may vote it a capital offence.

Do not trust any part of your work to others without carefully overlooking them; whatever faults they commit, you will be censured for; if you have forgotten any article which is indispensable for the day's dinner, request your employer to send one of the other servants for it. The cook must never quit her post, till her work is entirely finished.

It requires the utmost skill and contrivance to have all things done as they should be, and all done together, at that critical moment when the dinner bell sounds "to the banquet."

"A feast must be without a fault;
And, if 'tis not all right, 'tis naught."

But,
"Good nature will some failings overlook,
Forgive mischance, not errors of the cook:
As, if no salt is thrown about the dish;
Or nice crisp'd parsley scatter'd on the fish
Shall we in passion from our dinner fly,
And hopes of pardon to the cook deny,
For things which Mrs. Glass herself might oversee,
And all mankind commit as well as she?"

Such is the endless variety of culinary preparations, it would be as vain and fruitless a search, as that for the philosopher's stone, to expect to find a cook who is quite perfect in the operations of the spit, the stewpan, and the rolling-pin; you will as soon find a watchmaker, who can make, put together, and regulate every part of a watch.

"The universe cannot produce that cook who knows how to do every branch of cookery well, be his genius as great as possible."

Those who desire regularity in the service of their table, should have a dial of about twelve inches diameter, placed over the kitchen fireplace, carefully regulated, to keep time exactly with the clock in the hall or dining parlour; with a frame on one side, containing a taste table, of the peculiarities of the master's palate, and the particular rules and orders of his kitchen, and on the other side, of rewards given to those who attend to them, and for long and faithful service.

In small families, where a dinner is seldom given, a great deal of preparation is required, and the preceding day must be devoted to the business of the kitchen.

On these occasions a char-woman is often employed to do the dirty work, but we rather advise you to hire a cook to help to dress the dinner, this would be very little more expense, and the work got through much better.

When you have a very large entertainment to prepare, get your soups and sauces, forcemeats, &c. ready the day before; many made dishes may also be prepared the day before they are to go to table, but do not do them quite enough the first day, that they may not be overdone by warming up again.

Prepare every thing you can the day before the dinner, and order every thing else to be sent in early in the morning; if the tradesmen forget it, it will allow you time to send for it.

The pastry, jellies, &c. you may prepare while the broths are doing: then truss your game and poultry, and shape your collops, cutlets, &c. Nothing should go to table but what has indisputable pretensions to be eaten!

Put your made dishes in plates, and arrange them upon the dresser in regular order; next see that your roasts and boils are all nicely trimmed, trussed, &c. and quite ready for the spit or the pot.

Have your vegetables neatly cut, pared, picked, and clean washed in the cullender: provide a tin dish with partitions, to hold your fine herbs; onions and shallots, parsley, thyme, terragon, chervil, and burnet, minced very fine, and lemon peel grated, or cut thin, and chopped very small; pepper and salt ready mixed, and your spice-box and salt-cellar always ready for action, that every thing you want may be at hand for your stove-work, and not be scampering about the kitchen in a whirlpool of confusion, hunting after these trifles, while the dinner is waiting.

Nothing can be done in perfection, that must be done in a hurry; therefore, if you wish the dinner to be sent up to please your master and mistress, and do credit to yourself, set a high value on your character for punctuality: this shows the establishment is orderly, is extremely gratifying to the master and his guests, and is most praise-worthy in the attendants.

But, remember, you cannot obtain this desirable reputation, without good management in every respect; if you wish to insure ease and independence in the latter part of your life, you must not be unwilling to pay the price for which only they can be obtained, and earn them by a diligent and faithful performance of the duties of your station in your young days, which, if you steadily persevere in, you may depend upon ultimately receiving the reward your services deserve.

All duties are reciprocal; and if you hope to receive favour, endeavour to deserve it by showing yourself fond of obliging, and grateful when obliged; such behaviour will win regard and maintain it, enforce what is right, and excuse what is wrong.

Quiet steady perseverance is the only sure spring which you can safely depend upon to infallibly promote your progress on the road to independence.

If your employers do not immediately appear to be sensible of your endeavours to contribute your utmost to their comfort and interest, be not easily discouraged; persevere and do all in your power to make yourself useful.*

---

*N.B. If you will take half the pains to deserve the regard of your master, by being a good and faithful servant, you take to be considered a good fellow-servant, so many of you would not, in the decline of life, be left destitute of

Endeavour to promote the comfort of every individual in the family, let it be manifest that you are desirous to do rather *more* than what is required of you, than *less* than your duty: they merit little who perform merely what would be exacted: if you are desired to help in any business which may not strictly belong to your department, undertake it cheerfully, patiently, and conscientiously.

☞ The preceding remarks and advice to cooks, are extracted from the Cook's Oracle, a work which should be oftener in the hands of every Cook, but which I have seldom seen.

A WORD TO HEADS OF FAMILIES

It will be evident to you, my respected employers, that the foregoing observations are thrown together in a very crude and imperfect manner. The writer has no pretensions as a scholar, but considerable experience as a servant, and it was his wish, however poorly he may have succeeded in the attempt, to convey the result of that experience to his fellow servants for their instruction and guidance. If he has succeeded in the slightest degree, he humbly thinks it will be more readily received and read by servants, for whom it was exclusively intended, than if written in highflown terms, or by one among yourselves. You, my respected masters and mistresses, will reap the principal advantage of the diffusion of a knowledge of their duties among servants, whose ignorance is sometimes very troublesome. The writer, however, has farther endeavoured, in all cases, to enforce upon the minds of servants, in stating rules and duties, that "might is right"; that these rules are subject to modification and variation at your will and pleasure. "The servant is not greater

---

those comforts which age requires, nor have occasion to quote the saying that, "service is no inheritance," unless your own misconduct makes it so.

"The idea of being called a tell-tale has occasioned many good servants to shut their eyes against the frauds of fellow-servants. In the eye of the law, persons standing by and seeing a felony committed, which they could have prevented, are both equally guilty with those committing it."

than his master," neither are any rules or regulations; "new masters, new laws," and every servant must conform to those of the family where he takes up his residence, without demur or hesitation.

On the other hand a few words might be said to masters and mistresses, in behalf of those who are dependent on them for their present, and oftentimes for their eternal good. "The labourer is worthy of his hire," and should be treated in health or in sickness with pity and feeling; if it is necessary to place servants under strict surveillance, let them at least be treated as fellow beings and candidates for a future world. It would be presumption in me, a servant, to urge aught on this subject to my superiors, I beg leave therefore respectfully to conclude with the following extract in behalf of the cook and other servants, taken from the said Oracle.

"A good dinner is one of the greatest enjoyments of human life; and as the practice of cookery is attended with so many discouraging difficulties, so many disgusting and disagreeable circumstances, and even dangers, we ought to have some regard for those who encounter them, to procure us pleasure, and to reward their attention, by rendering their situation every way as comfortable and agreeable as we can. Mere money is a very inadequate compensation to a complete cook; he who has preached integrity to those in the kitchen may be permitted to recommend liberality to those in the parlour; they are indeed the sources of each other.

Depend upon it, "true self-love and social, are the same"; "do as you would be done by"; give those you are obliged to trust, every inducement to be honest, and no temptation to play tricks.

When you consider that a good servant eats no more than a bad one, how much more waste is occasioned by provisions being dressed in a slovenly and unskilful manner, and how much a good cook (to whom the conduct of the kitchen is confided) can save you by careful management, no housekeeper will hardly deem it an unwise speculation, it is certainly an amiable experiment, to invite the honesty and industry of domestics, by setting them an example of liberality; at least, show them, that "according to their pains, will be their gains." But trust not your servants with the secret of their own strength; importance of any kind, being what human frailty is least able to bear.

Avoid all approaches towards familiarity, which to a proverb is accompanied by contempt, and soon breaks the neck of obedience.

Servants are more likely to be praised into good conduct, than scolded out of bad; always commend them when they do right; to cherish the desire of pleasing in them, you must show them that you are pleased:—

> "Be to their faults a little blind,
> And to their virtues very kind."

By such conduct, ordinary servants will often be converted into good ones; few are so hardened as not to feel gratified when they are kindly and liberally treated.

It is a good maxim to select servants not younger than thirty; before that age, however comfortable you may endeavour to make them, their want of experience, and the hope of something still better, prevents their being satisfied with their present state. After they have had the benefit of experience, if they are tolerably comfortable, they will endeavour to deserve the smiles of even a moderately kind master, for fear they may change for the worse.

Life may indeed be very fairly divided into the seasons of hope and fear. In youth, we hope every thing may be right; in age we fear every thing will be wrong.

Do not discharge a good servant for a slight offense—

> "Bear and forbear, thus preached the stoic sages,
> And in two words include the sense of pages."—*Pope.*

Human nature is the same in all stations; if you can convince your servants, that you have a generous and considerate regard for their health and comfort, why should you imagine that they will be insensible to the good they receive?

Impose no commands but what are reasonable, nor reprove but with justice and temper; the best way to ensure which, is never to lecture them, till at least one day after they have offended you.

If they have any particular hardships to endure in your service, let them see that you are concerned for the necessity of imposing it.

If they are sick, remember you are their patron as well as their master; not only remit their labour, but give them all the assistance of food, physic, and every comfort in your power. Tender assiduity about an invalid is half a cure, it is a balsam to the mind, which has a most powerful effect on the body, soothes the sharpest pains, and strengthens beyond the richest cordial.

Ye, who think that to protect and encourage virtue, is the best preventative from vice, give your female servants liberal wages.

"Charity should begin at home,"—"prevention is preferable to cure," but I have no objection to see your names ornamenting the list of subscribers to foundling hospitals, and female penitentiaries.

To say nothing of the deleterious vapours and pestilential exhalations of the charcoal, which soon undermine the health of the heartiest, the glare of a scorching fire, and the smoke so baneful to the eyes and the complexion, are continual and inevitable dangers; and a cook must live in the midst of them, as a soldier on the field of battle, surrounded by bullets, and bombs, and Congreve's rockets, with this only difference, that for the first, every day is a fighting day, that her warfare is almost always without glory, and most praiseworthy achievements pass not only without reward, but frequently without even thanks; for the most consummate cook is, alas! seldom noticed by the master, or heard of by the guests; who, while they are eagerly devouring his turtle, and drinking his wine, care very little who dressed the one, or sent the other.

The greatest care should be taken by the man of fashion, that his cook's health be preserved.

Cleanliness, and a proper ventilation to carry off smoke and steam, should be particularly attended to in the construction of a kitchen; the grand scene of action, the fire place, should be placed where it may receive plenty of light. Hitherto the contrary has prevailed, and the poor cook is continually blasted with her own perspiration.

It is almost impossible for a cook to attend to the business of the kitchen with any certainty of perfection if employed in other household concerns. It is a service of such importance, and so difficult to perform even tolerably well, that it is sufficient to engross the entire attention of one person.

This is a maxim which is neither understood nor admitted in some families, where the cook is expected to be a house servant also, and coals are meted out to her by the quart, and butter by the ounce, &c.

If the master and mistress of a family will sometimes conde-scend to make an amusement of this art, they will escape a num-ber of disappointments, &c. which those who will not, must suf-fer, to the detriment of both their health and their fortune."

DIRECTIONS HOW TO MAKE
A FIRE OF LEHIGH COAL

And now, Joseph and David, I must address a few "last words" to you on the subject of making coal fires. Having put down all that need be said in respect to employers and servants in their conduct towards each other, I wish to add some very superior directions for making fires of what is called *anthracite* coal, oth-erwise called Lehigh, Rhode Island, or any hard coal.

Very few servants at first understand the method of kindling and continuing a fire of Lehigh coal, many will never learn, and many more from erroneous instructions, whilst they think they understand it, make but a bungling piece of work of it. I had prepared some observations on this subject to be inserted among the directions and receipts, but have omitted them in order to give room to the following full account and directions, and as our book is intended to be useful to servants, it must be granted that a knowledge how to make a Lehigh coal fire, when it is becoming so common in this country, is quite an acquisition.

I wish my fellow servants to read the rules very attentively. They are very humorous, but very true, and they lay down a plain and easy method for preparing and burning this kind of coal. These rules were first published in the "New York American,"—and people thought them a burlesque upon the use of this kind of fuel, but experience has made them acknowledge that they are most excellent and true, and hundreds have enjoyed the comforts of a hard coal fire made according to the writer's directions.

CHAPTER I.—OF BUYING AND BREAKING.*

1. Buy from the vessel, if possible; for a chaldron *there* is more than at the yard. And remember that every seller of coal is a cheat.

2. Stand by and see that large pieces only are put into the cart, for a cart of very large pieces, when broken up, makes a cart and a quarter of small ones.

3. Refuse a load that appears to contain dust, because Lehigh dust is clear waste, and enough in all conscience is made in the breaking.

4. Break the coal before housing it, unless you would have to break it yourself at the risk of either eye.

5. Do not be hoaxed out of a dollar for a hammer made expressly for the purpose of breaking Lehigh, the family axe is just as good.

6. Do not take a man from the yard with his patent hammer, to break your coal for you, unless you would pay twice what the job is worth, and what a dozen, in less than five minutes after the coal is dumped, will offer to do it for.

7. In breaking, see that each piece is broken by itself on the pavement, and not as is usual, on the mass, unless you wish to burn half the coal as powder.

8. Make the man who breaks carry in as fast as he breaks, whereby much dust will be saved.

9. Let the pieces into which it is broken be about as large as your fist, if your hand is rather a small one; otherwise, about the size of your wife's, provided her hand is something larger than common; or, about the size of a half-pint tumbler.

10. Watch the fellow who breaks, or he will not break half small enough—or he will break it on the mass—or he will use a

---

*This coal is sold by weight in Boston, and broken up at the yard, at an extra charge of fifty cents per ton.

bushel up as missiles against the boys, cows or pigs—or he will take care to wet it all in the gutter before he takes it up.

11. When the coal is in, proceed to the mystery of burning, which deserves a separate chapter. This subject, however, is better handled under the two heads, of kindling, and of replenishing and perpetuating.

CHAPTER II.—OF THE KINDLING

1. This is a great mystery, therefore proceed with caution and with a mind divested of all prejudice.

2. Let the grate be perfectly cleared of all foreign substances, and begin the fire at the *bottom.*

3. The best material for kindling is charcoal, unless perhaps dry hickory be preferred; the latter is much cheaper—not *absolutely* however, that I know of, but it is *relatively.* For, in relation to the cook, it may be affirmed that half the charcoal which you buy for kindling will go into the kitchen fire to save trouble. The cheapest method is this: buy a load of dry hickory, stipulate that it shall be large, have it sawed three times—the wood will now be in junks, which you may defy the cook to burn—split it up as fast as wanted and no faster. Some say that Liverpool is the cheapest kindler. It may be at six dollars a chaldron, but it is not at sixteen dollars: and then you must have wood to kindle the Liverpool.

4. Having got the kindling, proceed to the grate. Throw into it first live coals from the kitchen, then lay on the charcoal or hickory, be not too sparing,—then place loosely, and with the fingers, fair pieces of Schuylkill, Lehigh, or Rhode Island of the orthodox size. I advise the use of the fingers, because the work is done quicker than with the tongs, from which the smooth Schuylkill perpetually slips. Let the coal be piled as high as the grate will allow.

5. If you are in a hurry, put up the blower; if not, do not use it, for the hard coal kindles much better without forcing. The blower makes a quicker fire, but a worse one, for the outside of the coals is burned before the inside is even heated. When the blower is removed, the heat suddenly subsides; the coals

(Lehigh especially) are found encrusted with a white coating of hard ashes, which renders them almost incombustible, and the fire afterwards becomes very dull.

6. If the process of kindling fails, begin all over again. Failure most frequently proceeds from stinginess in the material of kindling. Better be prodigal of it than have the fire go out, and the grate all disembowelled a second time. Horresco referens.

7. The fire now being well kindled—but this is the subject of another chapter.

CHAPTER III.—OF REPLENISHING AND PERPETUATING

1. The fire being now well under way, it will need to be fed but three times during the day and evening. The first replenishing should take place immediately after breakfast, when the family breaks up, the gentlemen retreating to the counting-room, office, or study, and the ladies to their dressing-rooms; the second, about an hour before dinner; the third, a little into the evening.

2. If my readers are willing to be truly economical, let them replenish a fourth time, viz. at going to bed—which I call the *perpetuating process*. Since, if it be done properly, the fire need be kindled but once for the whole winter, say on the 1st day of November, and thus an immense amount of kindling matter may be saved.

3. The method of perpetuating is exceedingly simple, and consists merely in adding a few pieces of coal at 11 o'clock say, and then covering the whole with cinders and ashes, usque sat-ictatum—i.e. till you have shovelled up as much as the grate can bear. In the morning all you have to do, is to clap on the blower, and presto, the fire before you is red hot. Following this plan, my parlour has always been comfortable at breakfast.

4. Let not the ladies murmur: the grate can still be cleaned. When the servant first approaches the grate in the morning, every thing is calm, quiet, slumbering and cool—you would hardly believe the fire to be there: and the brass can therefore be polished without the least hindrance. And not till that is done should the blower be applied.

CHAPTER IV.—OF THE POKER

1. A judicious use of the poker is essential to the well-being of an anthracite fire. This is the most delicate part of the science of coal burning, and the strictest attention should be given to it. So nice a matter is this, that I am almost ready to say, that I can form my opinion of a man's intellect from his application of the poker as well as his pleading, preaching, or physicking.

2. An ignorant, meddlesome, or nervous person you will often see thrusting in the poker at all adventures, without rhyme or reason—as often marring as making the fire. In a cold winter day particularly, the poker should always be kept out of their reach. They are unworthy its honors.

3. The legitimate office of the poker, in the case of a hard coal fire, is to clear away the ashes which accumulate on the lower bars, and promote a free circulation of air. Not to quicken the blaze by breaking a large coal in pieces, or by changing the position of pieces, as in fires of Liverpool.

4. A fire should be poked when at its zenith—if you wait till it is much below that, your poking will only poke it out; the more you poke the less it will burn.

5. If the fire, from having been too long neglected, appear to be in a doubtful state, hesitating between life and death—*never touch a poker to it,* it will be the death of it—never stir it— scarce look or breathe upon it, but with the step of a ghost, clap on the blower, and if the vital spark be not wholly extinct, the air will find it out, and in a few moments blow it up to a generous heat—then gradually add fresh coal in small clean pieces, devoid of dust, and your fire is safe.—Servants never learn this mystery, they always fly to the poker in every case of distress, and by their stupid use of it, double their own labor and vex the mistress of the house.

6. This direction should be particularly observed in the morning, when a fire has been *perpetuated.* No coal should be added, nor the fire *touched,* till after the blower has been up and done its work. It will often be found, especially in the case of the Schuylkill coal, far preferable to Lehigh—that this alone will furnish a sufficient heat for the breakfast hour; which is a

demonstration that it is no waste, but a clear saving, to perpetu-
ate the fire in the manner laid down.

7. Many more niceties might be enumerated touching the
poker; but I refrain and willingly leave something to the imagi-
nation of the reader. I would conclude, as the preachers say,
with only one practical remark—that you will never have a good
anthracite fire, till you have broken your husband, a brother, or
wife, of the mischievous habit of poking. It is surely an unseemly
habit in itself, as well as an injurious one to the fire. It shows too
a meddlesome, prying, insinuating disposition; and I can never
help thinking, when I see one of this sort poking the coals, that
he only wants the opportunity to thrust himself into my private
affairs.

CHAPTER V.—CONTAINING MISCELLANIES

1. If the Savings Bank is a good thing in Wall-street, it is a
better thing in our own houses. If we save at home, we need not
put our money there, we shall be rich enough without money at
interest. We waste in nothing more than the use of hard coal.
The cinders which I see every day lying in the streets, nay
before my own door, would, if gathered up, afford fuel to many
a poor family; yet I confess that I do not see how the evil is to
be remedied. The cinders get so mingled with the ashes, that it
is difficult to separate them, and the servants will not do it. But
till a way is discovered of saving them, a Schuylkill may be a
clean and hot fire, but it will not be a cheap one. Of Liverpool
coal you can burn every atom.

2. The blower should questionless be the size of the whole
grate; but it should be used with discretion.

3. As to the form of grates, I think on the whole, that the
Lehigh grate with horizontal front bars, and rake ones for the
bottom, possesses the greatest advantages.—There is the greatest objection to one of the common Liverpool construction,
which is, that the floor of it, the bottom bars, are altogether too
thickly set. The ashes cannot fall through, but collect upon
them, deaden and finally extinguish the fire, while the coal is not
half consumed. In order to keep the fire a-going at all, there

must be a very frequent clearing away of the ashes with the poker. A practice to be deprecated, as it tends to generate the worst habits.

I had sketched the heads of a couple of chapters on the merits of anthracite in general, and on the relative excellences of Lehigh, Schuylkill, and Rhode Island, but I must defer them to some other time, and in the meanwhile I commend my readers to the kind care of a spirit-stirring Schuylkill grate.

CHAPTER VI.—OF THE THREE COALS AND THEIR ADVANTAGES OVER LIVERPOOL

1. As to the general merits of hard coal over Liverpool, or any other bituminous coal—and I place *cleanliness* at the very top of its virtues,—cleanliness as to smoke, dust, and smell. Were they at the same price, and of the same endurance, I should take without hesitation the hard coal, it is so infinitely cleaner. Burn Liverpool, and your clothes are smutted—your flesh begrimmed—your furniture dirtied—your walls blackened, and wherever there happens to be a crack, seamed with long tapering streaks of soot—your carpets soiled, and when taken up, if there are cracks in your floor, are found indelibly stained with corresponding lines of smut, to such a degree that you are defeated in your economical purpose of wearing them next year the wrong side up. I say nothing of the filthy smut that deposits itself on your books and papers—of the unnumbered cobwebs brought to light by the smoke and dust gathering on them, which might else have hung undiscerned for months or years— of those globules of pure greasy black in the shape of *polly-wogs* that go sailing round the room, and light on your shirt collar or cheek, where they are unwittingly rubbed in, while you, like Malvolio, cross-gartered, parade yourself in the streets, and wonder to see every one smile as he passes. And then, the stench of this vile coal, when a strong northwester, or whatever the wind is that nauseates the throat of your chimney, blows the smoke in Stygian puffs into your parlour and face—boh! suicide might be traced to it.

But burn anthracite, and the whole scene is changed. White-wash your parlours in the spring or autumn, and the white is just as fresh and pure at the end of a long winter as at first. After three months fire in my parlour, I have been unable to perceive the slightest dinginess in the walls, ceiling, or cornice.—A matter of the greatest consequence in those houses where the cornice has its oak leaves, rosettes, dentals, and nobody knows what more, of architectural ginger-bread work. For, by frequent white-washings, though done with ever so much care, and with the nicest Paris white, the fine sharp edges, graceful curves, and delicate cavities on which the beauty of the cornice wholly depends, are lost, being cased over or filled up by the muddy brush of the black white-washer. The *dust,* too, which hard coal makes, though light and fine, is clean and pure, and easily dislodged from the mantel-piece and furniture, without leaving the least trace of its presence. Its visibility, wherever it does light, serves also to keep the lady of the house on the alert, and the dusting-cloth in more frequent action. And as to *smell,* it has infinitely the preference over the bituminous coals. It savours of sulphur to be sure, and the associations are by no means agreeable: but so do the Congress waters smell of sulphur, and taste too, yet we travel 500 or 1000 miles to enjoy it. But the smell, however, cannot be denied to be a pure, wholesome, medical one, though perhaps now and then a little too strong, especially from the Schuylkill. The Rhode Island is remarkable for being wholly innocent of the fumes that proceed both from Lehigh and Schuylkill. A great merit surely.

2. As to durability. All kinds of hard coal stand the heat remarkably well. But I confess they do not stand it so well as I could wish. They do burn out. The best will consume away after a while. The truth is, that though a fire of Anthracite will, to be sure, last longer than one of Liverpool, yet a *chaldron* of anthracite will not last a whit longer than a *chaldron* of Liverpool. And the reason is, that while a peck of Liverpool makes as good a fire as is ordinarily wanted in the coldest weather, it takes a bushel of Anthracite. If a hard coal fire therefore lasts longer, it ought to, in all conscience, for it is four times as big. I state the case in round terms, but I am persuaded that they represent the truth very nearly: yet, if there is no great cheapness, there is great comfort in a hard coal fire, in its steadiness, constancy, and trustworthiness. Like a man of integrity and consistency, you always

know where to find it. It plays you no tricks, but maintains the same sober, equal demeanour. When you go out, if you just cast a look at the grate, provided you have studied the subject properly, you know just how long you can be gone and find a good fire when you return. You can tell with great exactness whether it will stand 2, 3, 4, 5, or 6 hours longer. But a Liverpool fire deceives you perpetually. You left perhaps a good fire and ample coal on, to last till you should get back; but when you enter your parlour, shivering with cold, all is black—the fire has either gone out, leaving the half-burnt coal all bridged over the grate; or, having found a vent through the superincumbent mass, the draught thus created has whistled it all away, in a manner altogether rapid, costly and provoking.

3. As to the Heat.—With a right furious draught, in a grate properly constructed, I believe that the hard coal in an equal quantity would yield a fiercer heat than Liverpool. But in a sluggish grate, where the hard coal burns slowly, it is with much ado that a *small* room can be kept warm with it, while Liverpool frequently renewed and judiciously poked, would drive you out of it. Take an equal weight of each and subject each to the highest draught, and I have no doubt that the anthracite would yield vastly more heat—more intense and for a longer period than Liverpool. It is said that the Rhode Island makes a hotter fire than either of the others, and from a short trial I am inclined to believe that it is true. It certainly makes more flame—much more—as the trial of it at M'Queen's furnace proved, and as my own experience has proved also. A fire of Rhode Island is, too, more beautiful than one of Lehigh or Schuylkill. The flame is indeed exceedingly beautiful. You see all sorts of colours issuing from the top of the fire and blending together; rose pink, purple, violet, red and blue, now separate and distinct, and now weaving together. What it is that occasions this I know not. It may be the same mysterious cause that produces in Newport and the neighbourhood of the mines the most beautiful women. Every one knows that a Newport lady and beauty are almost convertible terms. It is a singular coincidence too, and well worth noticing, that, as the external of Rhode Island coal is exceedingly unprepossessing while the flame is so beautiful, so nothing can be more dismal than the outward aspect of Newport, though so

much beauty lies hidden beneath. Philosophers might perhaps speculate profitably on these analogies.

4. But I begin to prose. Old age, however, must be allowed its privileges.

CHAPTER VII.—THE HARD COALS BRIEFLY CONTRASTED

I do not intend saying much on this part of my subject, because of Rhode Island I know but little, and there is not after all, perhaps, much to be said. Besides, it will be construed into a piece of sheer prejudice and ill-nature by the wives of stockholders, if I should exalt one coal to the injury of that in which their husbands hold stock. To avoid an evil like this I shall say but a word, and leave the subject. I am afraid, however, that I shall certainly bring the wrath of many down upon my head by what little I do say— for in one word I do think the Schuylkill is the best of the three, and for this reason, that it burns the easiest. Who says it does not, I freely say does not know whereof he affirms, or he is prejudiced, while I aver that I am free of all prejudice.

The Lehigh, under similar circumstances of draught, will grow dull and go out, while the Schuylkill would have burned freely.

The Schuylkill burns itself up much more perfectly than Lehigh, which will oftentimes go out, leaving the grate half full of half burnt coal.

In perpetuating the fire, the pre-eminence of Schuylkill is particularly observable, it keeps fire through the night much better than Lehigh.

In breaking, Schuylkill breaks hard, Lehigh harder, Rhode Island least hard. Comparing them with strict grammatical precision, Rhode Island is hard, Schuylkill harder, Lehigh hardest, both to break and burn.

As to price, Schuylkill and Lehigh are cheap, comparative wanting, Rhode Island cheapest.

In respect of beauty of fracture, that of Lehigh is clean and smooth, that of Schuylkill exceedingly brilliant, of Rhode Island hideously ugly.

As to combustion, that of Rhode Island is the most complete and the residue the least.

In regard to ashes and dirt, they are about alike: Lehigh ashes being whitest, Schuylkill darker, and Rhode Island darker still. Lehigh perhaps makes the least ashes, though it leaves the most of a hard incombustible cinder. And Rhode Island perhaps makes the most ashes, while as far as I have discerned it, leaves nothing unburnt.

Many other slight comparisons suggest themselves, but they would be even less to the purpose than those I have already indulged in.

It has been hardly fair, perhaps, to our neighbour of Rhode Island to bring her into the lists, as we have not probably had a fair specimen of it yet in the market. What we have had, it is well known was water-soaked, by no means in a fit state for the grate. But there is every reason to believe that when the mines have been somewhat further opened, and the coal has been properly exposed in the drying house, it will burn with even more facility than the Schuylkill. From the assurances of one who has burned it in this perfectly dry state, it cannot be doubted; and on his assurances, one of the above comparisons is grounded. If, therefore, it shall the next year be offered at six or seven dollars the chaldron, we may at length be in possession of a cheap as well as good fuel.

I tear myself, Messrs. Editors, reluctantly from this dark but delightful theme. If I thought you would print more I would write more, but your patience must be exhausted.

I will only say, in conclusion, that could I utter myself in the language of our first poet, now happily a citizen of our city, I should think it no profanation of my powers to employ them in singing the beauties of the many coloured Schuylkill.

AN AMATEUR.

MISCELLANEOUS OBSERVATIONS

COMPILED FOR THE USE OF HOUSE SERVANTS

Many well-meaning servants are ignorant of the best means of managing, and thereby waste as much as would maintain a small family, besides causing the mistress of the house much chagrin by their irregularity: and many families, from a want of method, have the appearance of chance rather than of regular system. To avoid this, the following hints may be useful as well as economical:—

Every article should be kept in that place best suited to it, as much waste may thereby be avoided, viz.

Vegetables will keep best on a stone floor, if the air be excluded.—Meat in a cold dry place.—Sugar and sweetmeats require a dry place; so does salt.—Candles cold, but not damp.—Dried meats, hams, &c. the same.—All sorts of seeds for puddings, saloop, rice, &c. should be close covered, to preserve from insects; but that will not prevent it, if long kept.

Bread is so heavy an article of expense, that all waste should be guarded against; and having it cut in the room will tend much to prevent it. It should not be cut until a day old. Earthen pans and covers keep it best.

Straw, to lay apples on, should be quite dry, to prevent a musty taste.

Large pears should be tied up by the stalk.

Basil, savoury, or knotted marjoram, or thyme, to be used when herbs are ordered; but with discretion, as they are very pungent.

The best means to preserve blankets from moths is to fold and lay them under the feather-beds that are in use; and they should be shaken occasionally. When soiled, they should be washed, not scoured.

Soda, by softening the water, saves a great deal of soap. It should be melted in a large jug of water, some of which pour into the tubs and boiler; and when the latter becomes weak, add more. The new improvement in soft soap is, if properly used, a saving of near half in quantity; and though sometimes dearer than the hard, reduces the price of washing considerably.

Many good laundresses advise soaping linen in warm water the night previous to washing, as facilitating the operation with less friction.

Soap should be cut with a wire or twine, in pieces that will make a long square when first brought in, and kept out of the air two or three weeks; for if it dry quick, it will crack, and when wet, break. Put it on a shelf, leaving a space between, and let it grow hard gradually. Thus, it will save a full third in the consumption.

Some of the lemons and oranges used for juice should be pared first, to preserve the peel dry; some should be halved, and when squeezed, the pulp cut out, and the outsides dried for grating. If for boiling in any liquid, the first way is best. When these fruits are cheap, a proper quantity should be bought and prepared as above directed, especially by those who live in the country, where they cannot always be had; and they are perpetually wanted in cookery.

When whites of eggs are used for jelly, or other purposes, contrive to have pudding, custard, &c. to employ the yolks also. Should you not want them for several hours, beat them up with a little water, and put them in a cool place, or they will be hardened and useless. It was a mistake of old, to think that the whites made cakes and puddings heavy; on the contrary, if beaten long and separately, they contribute greatly to give lightness, are an advantage to paste, and make a pretty dish, beaten with fruit, to set in cream, &c.

If copper utensils be used in the kitchen, the cook should be charged to be very careful not to let the tin be rubbed off, and to have them fresh done when the least defect appears, and never to put by any soup, gravy, &c. in them, or any metal utensil; stone and earthen vessels should be provided for those purposes, as likewise plenty of common dishes, that the table-set may not be used to put by cold meat.

Tin vessels, if kept damp, soon rust, which causes holes. Fenders, and tin linings of flowerpots, &c. should be painted every year or two.

Vegetables soon sour, and corrode metals and glazed red ware, by which a strong poison is produced. Some years ago, the death of several gentlemen was occasioned at Salt hill, (London,) by the cook sending a ragout to the table, which she had kept from the preceding day in a copper vessel badly tinned.

Vinegar, by its acidity, does the same, the glazing being of lead or arsenic.

To cool liquors in hot weather, dip a cloth in cold water, and wrap it round the bottle two or three times, then place it in the sun: renew the process once or twice.

The best way of scalding fruits, or boiling vinegar, is in a stone jar on a hot iron hearth; or by putting the vessel into a saucepan of water, called a water-bath.

If chocolate, coffee, jelly, gruel, bark, &c. be suffered to boil over, the strength is lost.

The cook should be charged to take care of jelly-bags, tapes for the collared things, &c. which, if not perfectly scalded, and kept dry, give an unpleasant flavour when next used.

Cold water thrown on cast-iron, when hot, will cause it to crack.

A cook must be quick and strong of sight: her hearing most acute, that she may be sensible when the contents of her vessels bubble, although they be closely covered, and that she may be alarmed before the pot boils over; her auditory nerve ought to discriminate (when several saucepans are in operation at the same time) the simmering of one, the ebullition of another, and the full-toned warbling of a third.

It is imperiously requisite that her organ of smell be highly susceptible of the various effluvia, that her nose may distinguish the perfection of aromatic ingredients, and that in animal substances it shall evince a suspicious accuracy between tenderness and putrefaction; above all, her olfactories should be tremblingly alive to mustiness and empyreuma.

It is from the exquisite sensibility of her palate, that we admire and judge of the cook; from the alliance between the olfactory and sapid organs it will be seen, that their perfection is indispensable.

Good manners have often made the fortune of many, who have had nothing else to recommend them: ill manners have as often marred the hopes of those who have had every thing else to advance them.

Dinner tables are seldom sufficiently lighted, or attended; an active waiter will have enough to do, to attend upon half a dozen good eaters: there should be half as many candles as there are guests, and their flame be about eighteen inches above the table, our foolish modern candelabras seem intended to illuminate the ceiling, rather than to give light on the plates, &c.

I am persuaded that no servant ever saved his master six-pence, but he found it in the end in his own pocket.

A surgeon may as well attempt to make an incision with a pair of sheers, or open a vein with an oyster knife, as a cook pretend to dress a dinner without proper tools.

When the pot is coming to a boil, there will always, from the cleanest meat and clearest water, rise a scum to the top of it; proceeding partly from the foulness of the meat, and partly from the water, this must be carefully taken off as soon as it rises; on this, depends the good appearance of all boiled things. When you have scummed well, put in some cold water, which will throw up the rest of the scum. The oftener it is scummed, and the cleaner the top of the water is kept, the cleaner will be the meat. If let alone, it soon boils down and sticks to the meat; which, instead of looking delicately white and nice, will have that coarse and filthy appearance we have too often to complain of, and the butcher and poulterer be blamed for the careless-ness of the cook in not scumming her pot.

In small families, we recommend block tin saucepans, &c. as lightest, and safest; if proper care is taken of them, and they are well dried after they are cleaned, they are by far the cheapest; the purchase of a new tin saucepan being little more than the expense of tinning a copper one.

Let the young cook never forget, that cleanliness is the chief cardinal virtue of the kitchen; the first preparation for roasting is to take care that the spit be properly cleaned with sand and water, nothing else. When it has been well scoured with this, dry it with a clean cloth. If spits are wiped clean, as soon as the meat is drawn from them, and while they are hot, a very little clean-ing will be required. The less the spit is passed through the meat the better, and before you spit it, joint it properly, especially necks and loins, that the carver may separate them easily and neatly, and take especial care it be evenly balanced on the spit, that its motion may be regular, and the fire operate equally on each part of it.

A cook must be as particular to proportion her fire to the business she has to do, as a chemist; the degree of heat most desirable for dressing the different sorts of food ought to be attended to with the utmost precision.

A good cook is as anxiously attentive to the appearance and colour of her roasts, as a court beauty is to her complexion at a birth-day ball.

Be very particular in frying, never to use any oil, butter, lard, or drippings, but what is quite clean, fresh, and free from salt. Any thing dirty spoils the look, any thing bad tasted or stale spoils the flavour, and salt prevents its browning.

There is nothing in which the difference between an elegant and an ordinary table is more seen, than in the dressing of vegetables, more especially of greens; they may be equally as fine at first, at one place as at another; but their look and taste are afterwards very different, entirely from the careless way in which they have been cooked.

Unripe vegetables are as insipid and unwholesome as unripe fruits.

If you wish to have vegetables delicately clean, put on your pot, make it boil, put a little salt in it, and skim it perfectly clean before you put in the greens, &c. which should not be put in till the water boils briskly; the quicker they boil, the greener they will be; when the vegetables sink, they are generally done enough, if the water has been constantly boiling. Take them up immediately, or they will lose their colour and goodness. Drain the water from them thoroughly before you send them to table. This branch of cookery requires the most vigilant attention.

If vegetables are a minute or two too long over the fire, they lose all their beauty and flavour.

Made dishes are nothing more than meat, poultry, or fish, stewed very gently till they are tender, with a thickened sauce poured over them.

Be careful to trim off all the skin, gristle, &c. that will not be eaten, and shape handsomely and of even thickness, the various articles which compose your made dishes; this is sadly neglected by common cooks; only stew them till they are just tender, and not do them to rags. Therefore, what you prepare the day before it is to be eaten, do not do quite enough the first day.

Woollen blankets or woollen clothes of any kind as well as furs, may be preserved from moths by sprinkling a little spirits of turpentine upon them, in the drawers or boxes where they are deposited during summer. The scent of the turpentine, on the woollens or furs, is immediately removed on their exposure to the air. Sheets of paper moistened with spirits of turpentine above or below the clothes, furs, &c. will have the effect of keeping off moths, but not so effectually as sprinkling.

When you open a bottle of catsup, essence of anchovy, &c. throw away the old cork, and stop it closely with a new cork that will fit it very tight. Use only the best superfine velvet taper corks.

Economy in corks is very unwise; in order to save a mere trifle, in the price of the cork, you run the risk of losing the valuable article it is intended to preserve. It is a vulgar error that a bottle must be well stopped, when the cork is forced down even with the mouth of it; this is a sure sign that the cork is too small, and it should be redrawn and a larger one put in.

The papering of a room, when soiled in spots as often happens, may be cleaned by a piece of brick loaf or biscuit, one or two days old. After gently rubbing till the bread is soiled, the soiled part of the bread should be chipped off, or a fresh piece taken; some caution is requisite not to injure the fabric of the paper-hanging, or the figures on it.

A CATALOG OF SELECTED DOVER
BOOKS IN ALL FIELDS OF INTEREST

CONCERNING THE SPIRITUAL IN ART, Wassily Kandinsky. Pioneering work by father of abstract art. Thoughts on color theory, nature of art. Analysis of earlier masters. 12 illustrations. 80pp. of text. 5⅜ x 8½.　　　　　0-486-23411-8

CELTIC ART: The Methods of Construction, George Bain. Simple geometric techniques for making Celtic interlacements, spirals, Kells-type initials, animals, humans, etc. Over 500 illustrations. 160pp. 9 x 12. (Available in U.S. only.)　　　　0-486-22923-8

AN ATLAS OF ANATOMY FOR ARTISTS, Fritz Schider. Most thorough reference work on art anatomy in the world. Hundreds of illustrations, including selections from works by Vesalius, Leonardo, Goya, Ingres, Michelangelo, others. 593 illustrations. 192pp. 7⅛ x 10¼.　　　　　0-486-20241-0

CELTIC HAND STROKE-BY-STROKE (Irish Half-Uncial from "The Book of Kells"): An Arthur Baker Calligraphy Manual, Arthur Baker. Complete guide to creating each letter of the alphabet in distinctive Celtic manner. Covers hand position, strokes, pens, inks, paper, more. Illustrated. 48pp. 8¼ x 11.　　　0-486-24336-2

EASY ORIGAMI, John Montroll. Charming collection of 32 projects (hat, cup, pelican, piano, swan, many more) specially designed for the novice origami hobbyist. Clearly illustrated easy-to-follow instructions insure that even beginning papercrafters will achieve successful results. 48pp. 8¼ x 11.　　　0-486-27298-2

BLOOMINGDALE'S ILLUSTRATED 1886 CATALOG: Fashions, Dry Goods and Housewares, Bloomingdale Brothers. Famed merchants' extremely rare catalog depicting about 1,700 products: clothing, housewares, firearms, dry goods, jewelry, more. Invaluable for dating, identifying vintage items. Also, copyright-free graphics for artists, designers. Co-published with Henry Ford Museum & Greenfield Village. 160pp. 8¼ x 11.　　　　　0-486-25780-0

THE ART OF WORLDLY WISDOM, Baltasar Gracian. "Think with the few and speak with the many," "Friends are a second existence," and "Be able to forget" are among this 1637 volume's 300 pithy maxims. A perfect source of mental and spiritual refreshment, it can be opened at random and appreciated either in brief or at length. 128pp. 5⅜ x 8½.　　　　　0-486-44034-6

JOHNSON'S DICTIONARY: A Modern Selection, Samuel Johnson (E. L. McAdam and George Milne, eds.). This modern version reduces the original 1755 edition's 2,300 pages of definitions and literary examples to a more manageable length, retaining the verbal pleasure and historical curiosity of the original. 480pp. 5¾₁₆ x 8¼.　　　　　0-486-44089-3

ADVENTURES OF HUCKLEBERRY FINN, Mark Twain, Illustrated by E. W. Kemble. A work of eternal richness and complexity, a source of ongoing critical debate, and a literary landmark, Twain's 1885 masterpiece about a barefoot boy's journey of self-discovery has enthralled readers around the world. This handsome clothbound reproduction of the first edition features all 174 of the original black-and-white illustrations. 368pp. 5⅜ x 8½.　　　　　0-486-44322-1

STICKLEY CRAFTSMAN FURNITURE CATALOGS, Gustav Stickley and L. & J. G. Stickley. Beautiful, functional furniture in two authentic catalogs from 1910. 594 illustrations, including 277 photos, show settles, rockers, armchairs, reclining chairs, bookcases, desks, tables. 183pp. 6½ x 9¼.   0-486-23838-5

AMERICAN LOCOMOTIVES IN HISTORIC PHOTOGRAPHS: 1858 to 1949, Ron Ziel (ed.). A rare collection of 126 meticulously detailed official photographs, called "builder portraits," of American locomotives that majestically chronicle the rise of steam locomotive power in America. Introduction. Detailed captions. xi+ 129pp. 9 x 12.   0-486-27393-8

AMERICA'S LIGHTHOUSES: An Illustrated History, Francis Ross Holland, Jr. Delightfully written, profusely illustrated fact-filled survey of over 200 American lighthouses since 1716. History, anecdotes, technological advances, more. 240pp. 8 x 10¾.
0-486-25576-X

TOWARDS A NEW ARCHITECTURE, Le Corbusier. Pioneering manifesto by founder of "International School." Technical and aesthetic theories, views of industry, economics, relation of form to function, "mass-production split" and much more. Profusely illustrated. 320pp. 6⅛ x 9¼. (Available in U.S. only.)   0-486-25023-7

HOW THE OTHER HALF LIVES, Jacob Riis. Famous journalistic record, exposing poverty and degradation of New York slums around 1900, by major social reformer. 100 striking and influential photographs. 233pp. 10 x 7⅞.   0-486-22012-5

FRUIT KEY AND TWIG KEY TO TREES AND SHRUBS, William M. Harlow. One of the handiest and most widely used identification aids. Fruit key covers 120 deciduous and evergreen species; twig key 160 deciduous species. Easily used. Over 300 photographs. 126pp. 5⅜ x 8½.   0-486-20511-8

COMMON BIRD SONGS, Dr. Donald J. Borror. Songs of 60 most common U.S. birds: robins, sparrows, cardinals, bluejays, finches, more—arranged in order of increasing complexity. Up to 9 variations of songs of each species.
Cassette and manual 0-486-99911-4

ORCHIDS AS HOUSE PLANTS, Rebecca Tyson Northen. Grow cattleyas and many other kinds of orchids—in a window, in a case, or under artificial light. 63 illustrations. 148pp. 5⅜ x 8½.   0-486-23261-1

MONSTER MAZES, Dave Phillips. Masterful mazes at four levels of difficulty. Avoid deadly perils and evil creatures to find magical treasures. Solutions for all 32 exciting illustrated puzzles. 48pp. 8¼ x 11.   0-486-26005-4

MOZART'S DON GIOVANNI (DOVER OPERA LIBRETTO SERIES), Wolfgang Amadeus Mozart. Introduced and translated by Ellen H. Bleiler. Standard Italian libretto, with complete English translation. Convenient and thoroughly portable—an ideal companion for reading along with a recording or the performance itself. Introduction. List of characters. Plot summary. 121pp. 5¼ x 8½. 0-486-24944-1

FRANK LLOYD WRIGHT'S DANA HOUSE, Donald Hoffmann. Pictorial essay of residential masterpiece with over 160 interior and exterior photos, plans, elevations, sketches and studies. 128pp. 9¹/₁ x 10¾.   0-486-29120-0

THE CLARINET AND CLARINET PLAYING, David Pino. Lively, comprehensive work features suggestions about technique, musicianship, and musical interpretation, as well as guidelines for teaching, making your own reeds, and preparing for public performance. Includes an intriguing look at clarinet history. "A godsend," *The Clarinet,* Journal of the International Clarinet Society. Appendixes. 7 illus. 320pp. 5$\frac{3}{8}$ x 8$\frac{1}{2}$. 0-486-40270-3

HOLLYWOOD GLAMOR PORTRAITS, John Kobal (ed.). 145 photos from 1926-49. Harlow, Gable, Bogart, Bacall; 94 stars in all. Full background on photographers, technical aspects. 160pp. 8$\frac{3}{8}$ x 11$\frac{1}{4}$. 0-486-23352-9

THE RAVEN AND OTHER FAVORITE POEMS, Edgar Allan Poe. Over 40 of the author's most memorable poems: "The Bells," "Ulalume," "Israfel," "To Helen," "The Conqueror Worm," "Eldorado," "Annabel Lee," many more. Alphabetic lists of titles and first lines. 64pp. 5$\frac{3}{16}$ x 8$\frac{1}{4}$. 0-486-26685-0

PERSONAL MEMOIRS OF U. S. GRANT, Ulysses Simpson Grant. Intelligent, deeply moving firsthand account of Civil War campaigns, considered by many the finest military memoirs ever written. Includes letters, historic photographs, maps and more. 528pp. 6$\frac{1}{8}$ x 9$\frac{1}{4}$. 0-486-28587-1

ANCIENT EGYPTIAN MATERIALS AND INDUSTRIES, A. Lucas and J. Harris. Fascinating, comprehensive, thoroughly documented text describes this ancient civilization's vast resources and the processes that incorporated them in daily life, including the use of animal products, building materials, cosmetics, perfumes and incense, fibers, glazed ware, glass and its manufacture, materials used in the mummification process, and much more. 544pp. 6$\frac{1}{8}$ x 9$\frac{1}{4}$. (Available in U.S. only.) 0-486-40446-3

RUSSIAN STORIES/RUSSKIE RASSKAZY: A Dual-Language Book, edited by Gleb Struve. Twelve tales by such masters as Chekhov, Tolstoy, Dostoevsky, Pushkin, others. Excellent word-for-word English translations on facing pages, plus teaching and study aids, Russian/English vocabulary, biographical/critical introductions, more. 416pp. 5$\frac{3}{8}$ x 8$\frac{1}{2}$. 0-486-26244-8

PHILADELPHIA THEN AND NOW: 60 Sites Photographed in the Past and Present, Kenneth Finkel and Susan Oyama. Rare photographs of City Hall, Logan Square, Independence Hall, Betsy Ross House, other landmarks juxtaposed with contemporary views. Captures changing face of historic city. Introduction. Captions. 128pp. 8$\frac{1}{4}$ x 11. 0-486-25790-8

NORTH AMERICAN INDIAN LIFE: Customs and Traditions of 23 Tribes, Elsie Clews Parsons (ed.). 27 fictionalized essays by noted anthropologists examine religion, customs, government, additional facets of life among the Winnebago, Crow, Zuni, Eskimo, other tribes. 480pp. 6$\frac{1}{8}$ x 9$\frac{1}{4}$. 0-486-27377-6

TECHNICAL MANUAL AND DICTIONARY OF CLASSICAL BALLET, Gail Grant. Defines, explains, comments on steps, movements, poses and concepts. 15-page pictorial section. Basic book for student, viewer. 127pp. 5$\frac{3}{8}$ x 8$\frac{1}{2}$. 0-486-21843-0

THE MALE AND FEMALE FIGURE IN MOTION: 60 Classic Photographic Sequences, Eadweard Muybridge. 60 true-action photographs of men and women walking, running, climbing, bending, turning, etc., reproduced from rare 19th-century masterpiece. vi + 121pp. 9 x 12. 0-486-24745-7

CATALOG OF DOVER BOOKS

ANIMALS: 1,419 Copyright-Free Illustrations of Mammals, Birds, Fish, Insects, etc., Jim Harter (ed.). Clear wood engravings present, in extremely lifelike poses, over 1,000 species of animals. One of the most extensive pictorial sourcebooks of its kind. Captions. Index. 284pp. 9 x 12.   0-486-23766-4

1001 QUESTIONS ANSWERED ABOUT THE SEASHORE, N. J. Berrill and Jacquelyn Berrill. Queries answered about dolphins, sea snails, sponges, starfish, fishes, shore birds, many others. Covers appearance, breeding, growth, feeding, much more. 305pp. 5¼ x 8¼.   0-486-23366-9

ATTRACTING BIRDS TO YOUR YARD, William J. Weber. Easy-to-follow guide offers advice on how to attract the greatest diversity of birds: birdhouses, feeders, water and waterers, much more. 96pp. 5³⁄₁₆ x 8¼.   0-486-28927-3

MEDICINAL AND OTHER USES OF NORTH AMERICAN PLANTS: A Historical Survey with Special Reference to the Eastern Indian Tribes, Charlotte Erichsen-Brown. Chronological historical citations document 500 years of usage of plants, trees, shrubs native to eastern Canada, northeastern U.S. Also complete identifying information. 343 illustrations. 544pp. 6½ x 9¼.   0-486-25951-X

STORYBOOK MAZES, Dave Phillips. 23 stories and mazes on two-page spreads: Wizard of Oz, Treasure Island, Robin Hood, etc. Solutions. 64pp. 8¼ x 11.
                                                                                0-486-23628-5

AMERICAN NEGRO SONGS: 230 Folk Songs and Spirituals, Religious and Secular, John W. Work. This authoritative study traces the African influences of songs sung and played by black Americans at work, in church, and as entertainment. The author discusses the lyric significance of such songs as "Swing Low, Sweet Chariot," "John Henry," and others and offers the words and music for 230 songs. Bibliography. Index of Song Titles. 272pp. 6½ x 9¼.   0-486-40271-1

MOVIE-STAR PORTRAITS OF THE FORTIES, John Kobal (ed.). 163 glamor, studio photos of 106 stars of the 1940s: Rita Hayworth, Ava Gardner, Marlon Brando, Clark Gable, many more. 176pp. 8⅜ x 11¼.   0-486-23546-7

YEKL and THE IMPORTED BRIDEGROOM AND OTHER STORIES OF YIDDISH NEW YORK, Abraham Cahan. Film Hester Street based on *Yekl* (1896). Novel, other stories among first about Jewish immigrants on N.Y.'s East Side. 240pp. 5⅜ x 8½.   0-486-22427-9

SELECTED POEMS, Walt Whitman. Generous sampling from *Leaves of Grass*. Twenty-four poems include "I Hear America Singing," "Song of the Open Road," "I Sing the Body Electric," "When Lilacs Last in the Dooryard Bloom'd," "O Captain! My Captain!"—all reprinted from an authoritative edition. Lists of titles and first lines. 128pp. 5³⁄₁₆ x 8¼.   0-486-26878-0

SONGS OF EXPERIENCE: Facsimile Reproduction with 26 Plates in Full Color, William Blake. 26 full-color plates from a rare 1826 edition. Includes "The Tyger," "London," "Holy Thursday," and other poems. Printed text of poems. 48pp. 5¼ x 7.
                                                                                0-486-24636-1

THE BEST TALES OF HOFFMANN, E. T. A. Hoffmann. 10 of Hoffmann's most important stories: "Nutcracker and the King of Mice," "The Golden Flowerpot," etc. 458pp. 5⅜ x 8½.   0-486-21793-0

THE BOOK OF TEA, Kakuzo Okakura. Minor classic of the Orient: entertaining, charming explanation, interpretation of traditional Japanese culture in terms of tea ceremony. 94pp. 5⅜ x 8½.   0-486-20070-1

FRENCH STORIES/CONTES FRANÇAIS: A Dual-Language Book, Wallace Fowlie. Ten stories by French masters, Voltaire to Camus: "Micromegas" by Voltaire; "The Atheist's Mass" by Balzac; "Minuet" by de Maupassant; "The Guest" by Camus, six more. Excellent English translations on facing pages. Also French-English vocabulary list, exercises, more. 352pp. 5⅜ x 8½. 0-486-26443-2

CHICAGO AT THE TURN OF THE CENTURY IN PHOTOGRAPHS: 122 Historic Views from the Collections of the Chicago Historical Society, Larry A. Viskochil. Rare large-format prints offer detailed views of City Hall, State Street, the Loop, Hull House, Union Station, many other landmarks, circa 1904-1913. Introduction. Captions. Maps. 144pp. 9⅜ x 12¼. 0-486-24656-6

OLD BROOKLYN IN EARLY PHOTOGRAPHS, 1865-1929, William Lee Younger. Luna Park, Gravesend race track, construction of Grand Army Plaza, moving of Hotel Brighton, etc. 157 previously unpublished photographs. 165pp. 8⅞ x 11¾. 0-486-23587-4

THE MYTHS OF THE NORTH AMERICAN INDIANS, Lewis Spence. Rich anthology of the myths and legends of the Algonquins, Iroquois, Pawnees and Sioux, prefaced by an extensive historical and ethnological commentary. 36 illustrations. 480pp. 5⅜ x 8½. 0-486-25967-6

AN ENCYCLOPEDIA OF BATTLES: Accounts of Over 1,560 Battles from 1479 B.C. to the Present, David Eggenberger. Essential details of every major battle in recorded history from the first battle of Megiddo in 1479 B.C. to Grenada in 1984. List of Battle Maps. New Appendix covering the years 1967-1984. Index. 99 illustrations. 544pp. 6½ x 9¼. 0-486-24913-1

SAILING ALONE AROUND THE WORLD, Captain Joshua Slocum. First man to sail around the world, alone, in small boat. One of great feats of seamanship told in delightful manner. 67 illustrations. 294pp. 5⅜ x 8½. 0-486-20326-3

ANARCHISM AND OTHER ESSAYS, Emma Goldman. Powerful, penetrating, prophetic essays on direct action, role of minorities, prison reform, puritan hypocrisy, violence, etc. 271pp. 5⅜ x 8½. 0-486-22484-8

MYTHS OF THE HINDUS AND BUDDHISTS, Ananda K. Coomaraswamy and Sister Nivedita. Great stories of the epics; deeds of Krishna, Shiva, taken from puranas, Vedas, folk tales; etc. 32 illustrations. 400pp. 5⅜ x 8½. 0-486-21759-0

MY BONDAGE AND MY FREEDOM, Frederick Douglass. Born a slave, Douglass became outspoken force in antislavery movement. The best of Douglass' autobiographies. Graphic description of slave life. 464pp. 5⅜ x 8½. 0-486-22457-0

FOLLOWING THE EQUATOR: A Journey Around the World, Mark Twain. Fascinating humorous account of 1897 voyage to Hawaii, Australia, India, New Zealand, etc. Ironic, bemused reports on peoples, customs, climate, flora and fauna, politics, much more. 197 illustrations. 720pp. 5⅜ x 8½. 0-486-26113-1

THE PEOPLE CALLED SHAKERS, Edward D. Andrews. Definitive study of Shakers: origins, beliefs, practices, dances, social organization, furniture and crafts, etc. 33 illustrations. 351pp. 5⅜ x 8½. 0-486-21081-2

THE MYTHS OF GREECE AND ROME, H. A. Guerber. A classic of mythology, generously illustrated, long prized for its simple, graphic, accurate retelling of the principal myths of Greece and Rome, and for its commentary on their origins and significance. With 64 illustrations by Michelangelo, Raphael, Titian, Rubens, Canova, Bernini and others. 480pp. 5⅜ x 8½. 0-486-27584-1

PSYCHOLOGY OF MUSIC, Carl E. Seashore. Classic work discusses music as a medium from psychological viewpoint. Clear treatment of physical acoustics, auditory apparatus, sound perception, development of musical skills, nature of musical feeling, host of other topics. 88 figures. 408pp. 5⅜ x 8½. 0-486-21851-1

LIFE IN ANCIENT EGYPT, Adolf Erman. Fullest, most thorough, detailed older account with much not in more recent books, domestic life, religion, magic, medicine, commerce, much more. Many illustrations reproduce tomb paintings, carvings, hieroglyphs, etc. 597pp. 5⅜ x 8½. 0-486-22632-8

SUNDIALS, Their Theory and Construction, Albert Waugh. Far and away the best, most thorough coverage of ideas, mathematics concerned, types, construction, adjusting anywhere. Simple, nontechnical treatment allows even children to build several of these dials. Over 100 illustrations. 230pp. 5⅜ x 8½. 0-486-22947-5

THEORETICAL HYDRODYNAMICS, L. M. Milne-Thomson. Classic exposition of the mathematical theory of fluid motion, applicable to both hydrodynamics and aerodynamics. Over 600 exercises. 768pp. 6⅛ x 9¼. 0-486-68970-0

OLD-TIME VIGNETTES IN FULL COLOR, Carol Belanger Grafton (ed.). Over 390 charming, often sentimental illustrations, selected from archives of Victorian graphics–pretty women posing, children playing, food, flowers, kittens and puppies, smiling cherubs, birds and butterflies, much more. All copyright free. 48pp. 9¼ x 12¼. 0-486-27269-9

PERSPECTIVE FOR ARTISTS, Rex Vicat Cole. Depth, perspective of sky and sea, shadows, much more, not usually covered. 391 diagrams, 81 reproductions of drawings and paintings. 279pp. 5⅜ x 8½. 0-486-22487-2

DRAWING THE LIVING FIGURE, Joseph Sheppard. Innovative approach to artistic anatomy focuses on specifics of surface anatomy, rather than muscles and bones. Over 170 drawings of live models in front, back and side views, and in widely varying poses. Accompanying diagrams. 177 illustrations. Introduction. Index. 144pp. 8⅜ x11¼. 0-486-26723-7

GOTHIC AND OLD ENGLISH ALPHABETS: 100 Complete Fonts, Dan X. Solo. Add power, elegance to posters, signs, other graphics with 100 stunning copyright-free alphabets: Blackstone, Dolbey, Germania, 97 more–including many lower-case, numerals, punctuation marks. 104pp. 8⅛ x 11. 0-486-24695-7

THE BOOK OF WOOD CARVING, Charles Marshall Sayers. Finest book for beginners discusses fundamentals and offers 34 designs. "Absolutely first rate . . . well thought out and well executed."–E. J. Tangerman. 118pp. 7¾ x 10⅝. 0-486-23654-4

ILLUSTRATED CATALOG OF CIVIL WAR MILITARY GOODS: Union Army Weapons, Insignia, Uniform Accessories, and Other Equipment, Schuyler, Hartley, and Graham. Rare, profusely illustrated 1846 catalog includes Union Army uniform and dress regulations, arms and ammunition, coats, insignia, flags, swords, rifles, etc. 226 illustrations. 160pp. 9 x 12. 0-486-24939-5

WOMEN'S FASHIONS OF THE EARLY 1900s: An Unabridged Republication of "New York Fashions, 1909," National Cloak & Suit Co. Rare catalog of mail-order fashions documents women's and children's clothing styles shortly after the turn of the century. Captions offer full descriptions, prices. Invaluable resource for fashion, costume historians. Approximately 725 illustrations. 128pp. 8⅜ x 11¼. 0-486-27276-1

HOW TO DO BEADWORK, Mary White. Fundamental book on craft from simple projects to five-bead chains and woven works. 106 illustrations. 142pp. 5⅜ x 8. 0-486-20697-1

THE 1912 AND 1915 GUSTAV STICKLEY FURNITURE CATALOGS, Gustav Stickley. With over 200 detailed illustrations and descriptions, these two catalogs are essential reading and reference materials and identification guides for Stickley furniture. Captions cite materials, dimensions and prices. 112pp. 6½ x 9¼. 0-486-26676-1

EARLY AMERICAN LOCOMOTIVES, John H. White, Jr. Finest locomotive engravings from early 19th century: historical (1804–74), main-line (after 1870), special, foreign, etc. 147 plates. 142pp. 11⅜ x 8¼. 0-486-22772-3

LITTLE BOOK OF EARLY AMERICAN CRAFTS AND TRADES, Peter Stockham (ed.). 1807 children's book explains crafts and trades: baker, hatter, cooper, potter, and many others. 23 copperplate illustrations. 140pp. 4⅝ x 6. 0-486-23336-7

VICTORIAN FASHIONS AND COSTUMES FROM HARPER'S BAZAR, 1867–1898, Stella Blum (ed.). Day costumes, evening wear, sports clothes, shoes, hats, other accessories in over 1,000 detailed engravings. 320pp. 9⅜ x 12¼. 0-486-22990-4

THE LONG ISLAND RAIL ROAD IN EARLY PHOTOGRAPHS, Ron Ziel. Over 220 rare photos, informative text document origin (1844) and development of rail service on Long Island. Vintage views of early trains, locomotives, stations, passengers, crews, much more. Captions. 8⅞ x 11¾. 0-486-26301-0

VOYAGE OF THE LIBERDADE, Joshua Slocum. Great 19th-century mariner's thrilling, first-hand account of the wreck of his ship off South America, the 35-foot boat he built from the wreckage, and its remarkable voyage home. 128pp. 5⅜ x 8½. 0-486-40022-0

TEN BOOKS ON ARCHITECTURE, Vitruvius. The most important book ever written on architecture. Early Roman aesthetics, technology, classical orders, site selection, all other aspects. Morgan translation. 331pp. 5⅜ x 8½. 0-486-20645-9

THE HUMAN FIGURE IN MOTION, Eadweard Muybridge. More than 4,500 stopped-action photos, in action series, showing undraped men, women, children jumping, lying down, throwing, sitting, wrestling, carrying, etc. 390pp. 7⅞ x 10⅝. 0-486-20204-6 Clothbd.

TREES OF THE EASTERN AND CENTRAL UNITED STATES AND CANADA, William M. Harlow. Best one-volume guide to 140 trees. Full descriptions, woodlore, range, etc. Over 600 illustrations. Handy size. 288pp. 4½ x 6⅜. 0-486-20395-6

GROWING AND USING HERBS AND SPICES, Milo Miloradovich. Versatile handbook provides all the information needed for cultivation and use of all the herbs and spices available in North America. 4 illustrations. Index. Glossary. 236pp. 5⅜ x 8½. 0-486-25058-X

BIG BOOK OF MAZES AND LABYRINTHS, Walter Shepherd. 50 mazes and labyrinths in all–classical, solid, ripple, and more–in one great volume. Perfect inexpensive puzzler for clever youngsters. Full solutions. 112pp. 8⅛ x 11. 0-486-22951-3

PIANO TUNING, J. Cree Fischer. Clearest, best book for beginner, amateur. Simple repairs, raising dropped notes, tuning by easy method of flattened fifths. No previous skills needed. 4 illustrations. 201pp. 5⅜ x 8½. 0-486-23267-0

CATALOG OF DOVER BOOKS

LIGHT AND SHADE: A Classic Approach to Three-Dimensional Drawing, Mrs. Mary P. Merrifield. Handy reference clearly demonstrates principles of light and shade by revealing effects of common daylight, sunshine, and candle or artificial light on geometrical solids. 13 plates. 64pp. 5⅜ x 8½. 0-486-44143-1

ASTROLOGY AND ASTRONOMY: A Pictorial Archive of Signs and Symbols, Ernst and Johanna Lehner. Treasure trove of stories, lore, and myth, accompanied by more than 300 rare illustrations of planets, the Milky Way, signs of the zodiac, comets, meteors, and other astronomical phenomena. 192pp. 8⅜ x 11. 0-486-43981-X

JEWELRY MAKING: Techniques for Metal, Tim McCreight. Easy-to-follow instructions and carefully executed illustrations describe tools and techniques, use of gems and enamels, wire inlay, casting, and other topics. 72 line illustrations and diagrams. 176pp. 8¼ x 10⅞. 0-486-44043-5

MAKING BIRDHOUSES: Easy and Advanced Projects, Gladstone Califf. Easy-to-follow instructions include diagrams for everything from a one-room house for bluebirds to a forty-two-room structure for purple martins. 56 plates; 4 figures. 80pp. 8¾ x 6⅜. 0-486-44183-0

LITTLE BOOK OF LOG CABINS: How to Build and Furnish Them, William S. Wicks. Handy how-to manual, with instructions and illustrations for building cabins in the Adirondack style, fireplaces, stairways, furniture, beamed ceilings, and more. 102 line drawings. 96pp. 8¾ x 6⅜. 0-486-44259-4

THE SEASONS OF AMERICA PAST, Eric Sloane. From "sugaring time" and strawberry picking to Indian summer and fall harvest, a whole year's activities described in charming prose and enhanced with 79 of the author's own illustrations. 160pp. 8¼ x 11. 0-486-44220-9

THE METROPOLIS OF TOMORROW, Hugh Ferriss. Generous, prophetic vision of the metropolis of the future, as perceived in 1929. Powerful illustrations of towering structures, wide avenues, and rooftop parks–all features in many of today's modern cities. 59 illustrations. 144pp. 8¼ x 11. 0-486-43727-2

THE PATH TO ROME, Hilaire Belloc. This 1902 memoir abounds in lively vignettes from a vanished time, recounting a pilgrimage on foot across the Alps and Apennines in order to "see all Europe which the Christian Faith has saved." 77 of the author's original line drawings complement his sparkling prose. 272pp. 5⅜ x 8½. 0-486-44001-X

THE HISTORY OF RASSELAS: Prince of Abissinia, Samuel Johnson. Distinguished English writer attacks eighteenth-century optimism and man's unrealistic estimates of what life has to offer. 112pp. 5⅜ x 8½. 0-486-44094-X

A VOYAGE TO ARCTURUS, David Lindsay. A brilliant flight of pure fancy, where wild creatures crowd the fantastic landscape and demented torturers dominate victims with their bizarre mental powers. 272pp. 5⅜ x 8½. 0-486-44198-9